MARVEL® GRAPHIC NOVEL

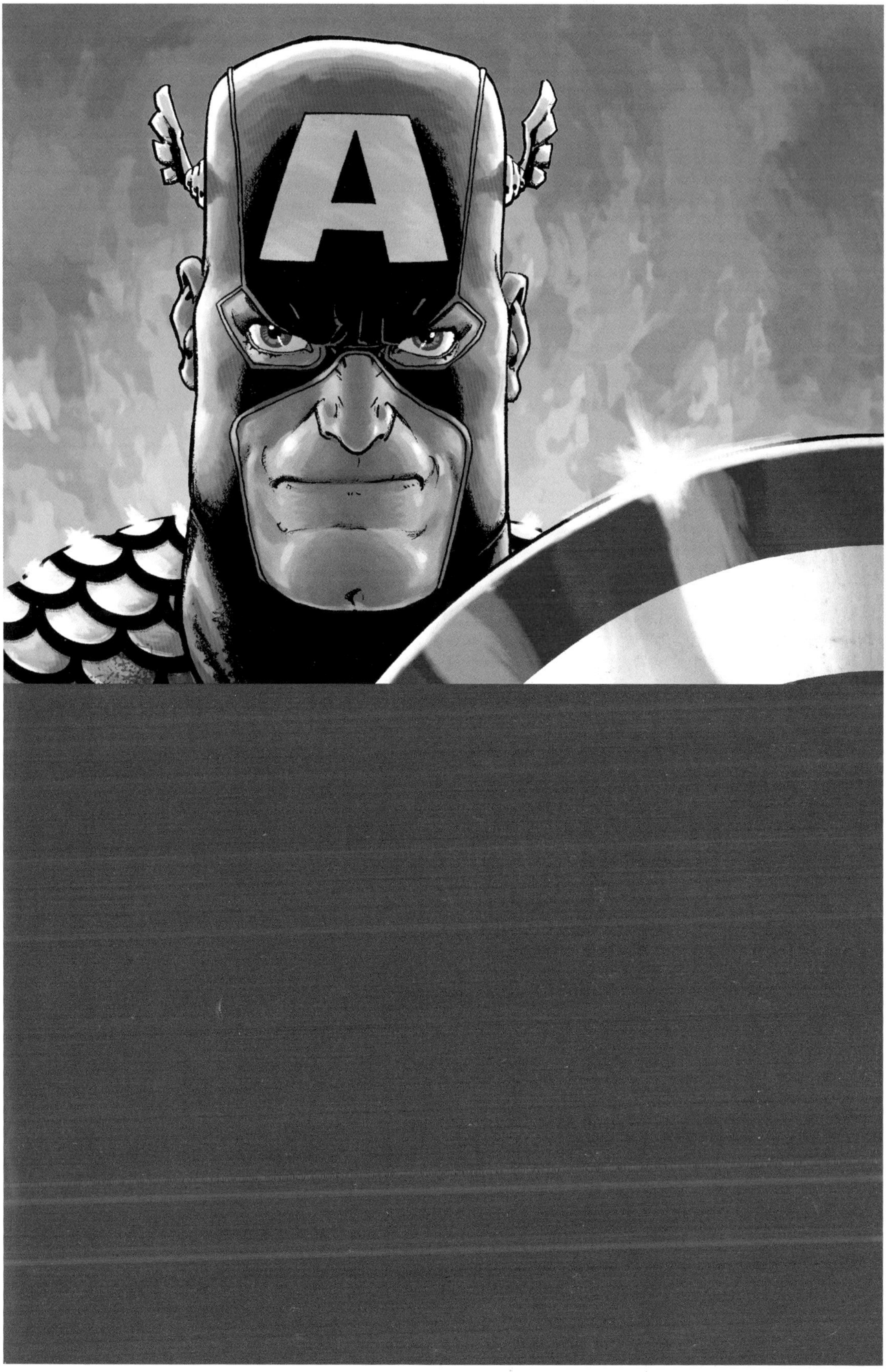

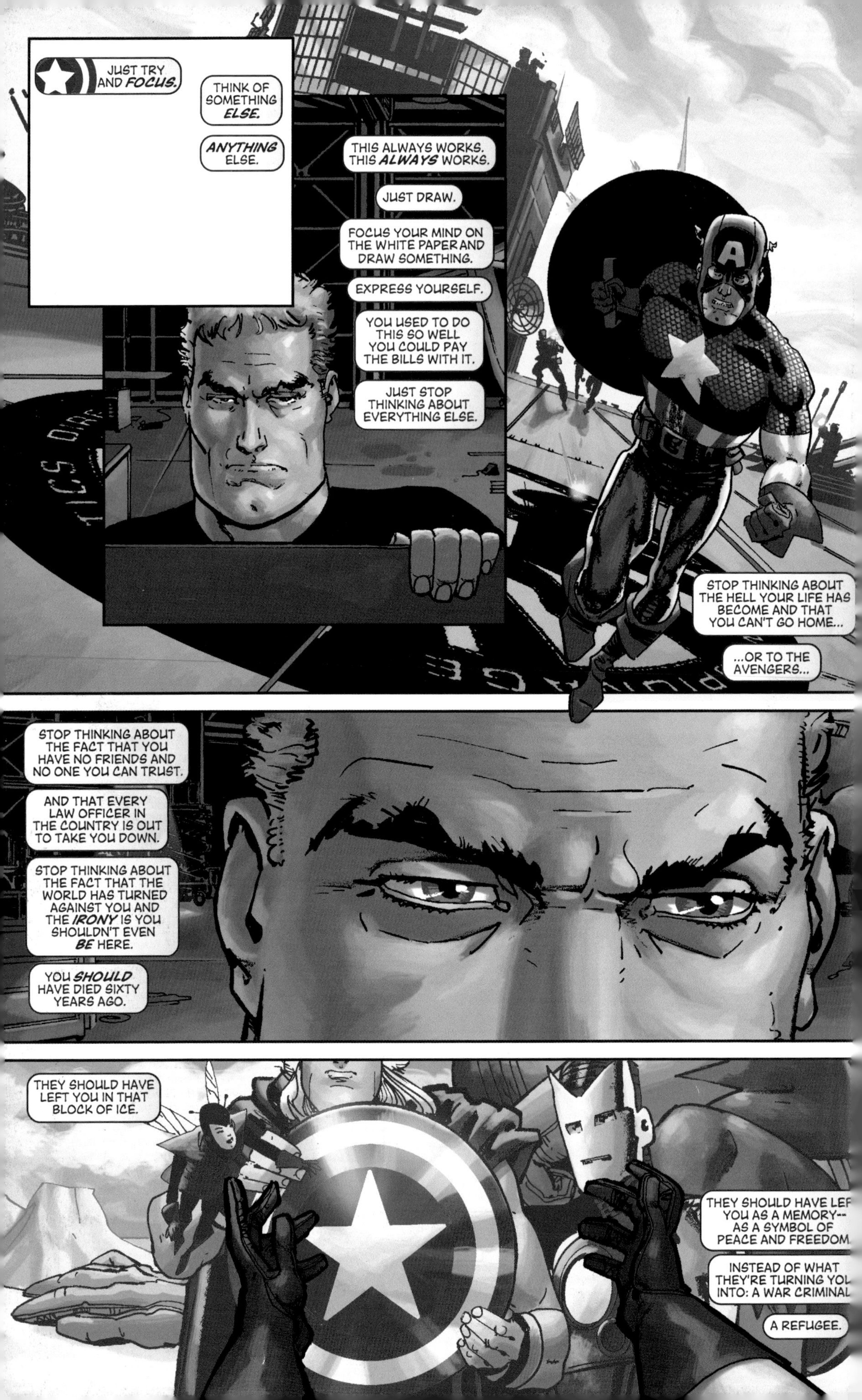
JUST TRY AND FOCUS.
THINK OF SOMETHING ELSE.
ANYTHING ELSE.
THIS ALWAYS WORKS. THIS ALWAYS WORKS.
JUST DRAW.
FOCUS YOUR MIND ON THE WHITE PAPER AND DRAW SOMETHING.
EXPRESS YOURSELF.
YOU USED TO DO THIS SO WELL YOU COULD PAY THE BILLS WITH IT.
JUST STOP THINKING ABOUT EVERYTHING ELSE.
STOP THINKING ABOUT THE HELL YOUR LIFE HAS BECOME AND THAT YOU CAN'T GO HOME...
...OR TO THE AVENGERS...
STOP THINKING ABOUT THE FACT THAT YOU HAVE NO FRIENDS AND NO ONE YOU CAN TRUST.
AND THAT EVERY LAW OFFICER IN THE COUNTRY IS OUT TO TAKE YOU DOWN.
STOP THINKING ABOUT THE FACT THAT THE WORLD HAS TURNED AGAINST YOU AND THE IRONY IS YOU SHOULDN'T EVEN BE HERE.
YOU SHOULD HAVE DIED SIXTY YEARS AGO.
THEY SHOULD HAVE LEFT YOU IN THAT BLOCK OF ICE.
THEY SHOULD HAVE LEF YOU AS A MEMORY-- AS A SYMBOL OF PEACE AND FREEDOM.
INSTEAD OF WHAT THEY'RE TURNING YO INTO: A WAR CRIMINAL
A REFUGEE.

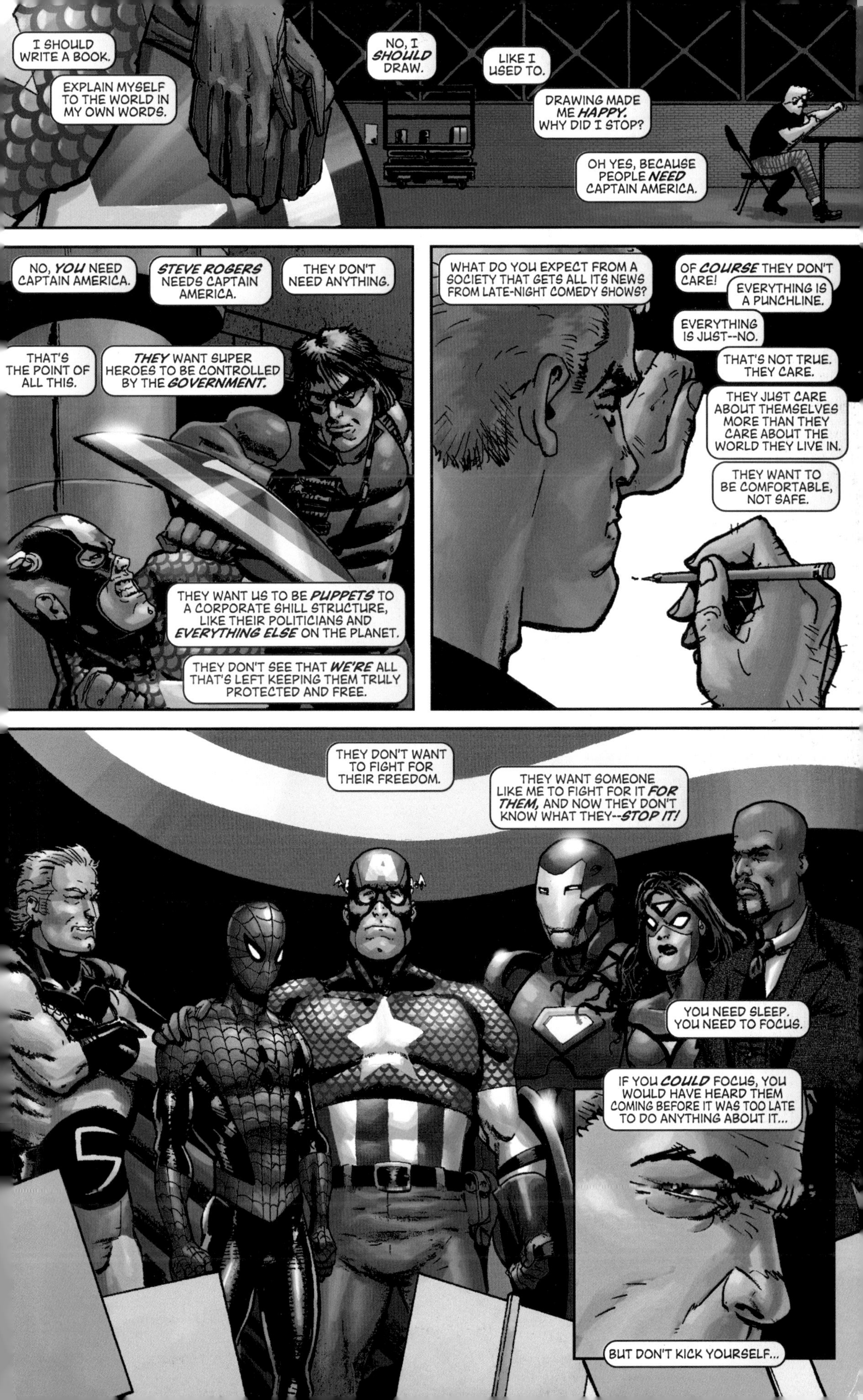
I SHOULD WRITE A BOOK.
EXPLAIN MYSELF TO THE WORLD IN MY OWN WORDS.
NO, I SHOULD DRAW.
LIKE I USED TO.
DRAWING MADE ME HAPPY. WHY DID I STOP?
OH YES, BECAUSE PEOPLE NEED CAPTAIN AMERICA.
NO, YOU NEED CAPTAIN AMERICA.
STEVE ROGERS NEEDS CAPTAIN AMERICA.
THEY DON'T NEED ANYTHING.
THAT'S THE POINT OF ALL THIS.
THEY WANT SUPER HEROES TO BE CONTROLLED BY THE GOVERNMENT.
THEY WANT US TO BE PUPPETS TO A CORPORATE SHILL STRUCTURE, LIKE THEIR POLITICIANS AND EVERYTHING ELSE ON THE PLANET.
THEY DON'T SEE THAT WE'RE ALL THAT'S LEFT KEEPING THEM TRULY PROTECTED AND FREE.
WHAT DO YOU EXPECT FROM A SOCIETY THAT GETS ALL ITS NEWS FROM LATE-NIGHT COMEDY SHOWS?
OF COURSE THEY DON'T CARE!
EVERYTHING IS A PUNCHLINE.
EVERYTHING IS JUST--NO.
THAT'S NOT TRUE. THEY CARE.
THEY JUST CARE ABOUT THEMSELVES MORE THAN THEY CARE ABOUT THE WORLD THEY LIVE IN.
THEY WANT TO BE COMFORTABLE, NOT SAFE.
THEY DON'T WANT TO FIGHT FOR THEIR FREEDOM.
THEY WANT SOMEONE LIKE ME TO FIGHT FOR IT FOR THEM, AND NOW THEY DON'T KNOW WHAT THEY--STOP IT!
YOU NEED SLEEP. YOU NEED TO FOCUS.
IF YOU COULD FOCUS, YOU WOULD HAVE HEARD THEM COMING BEFORE IT WAS TOO LATE TO DO ANYTHING ABOUT IT...
BUT DON'T KICK YOURSELF...

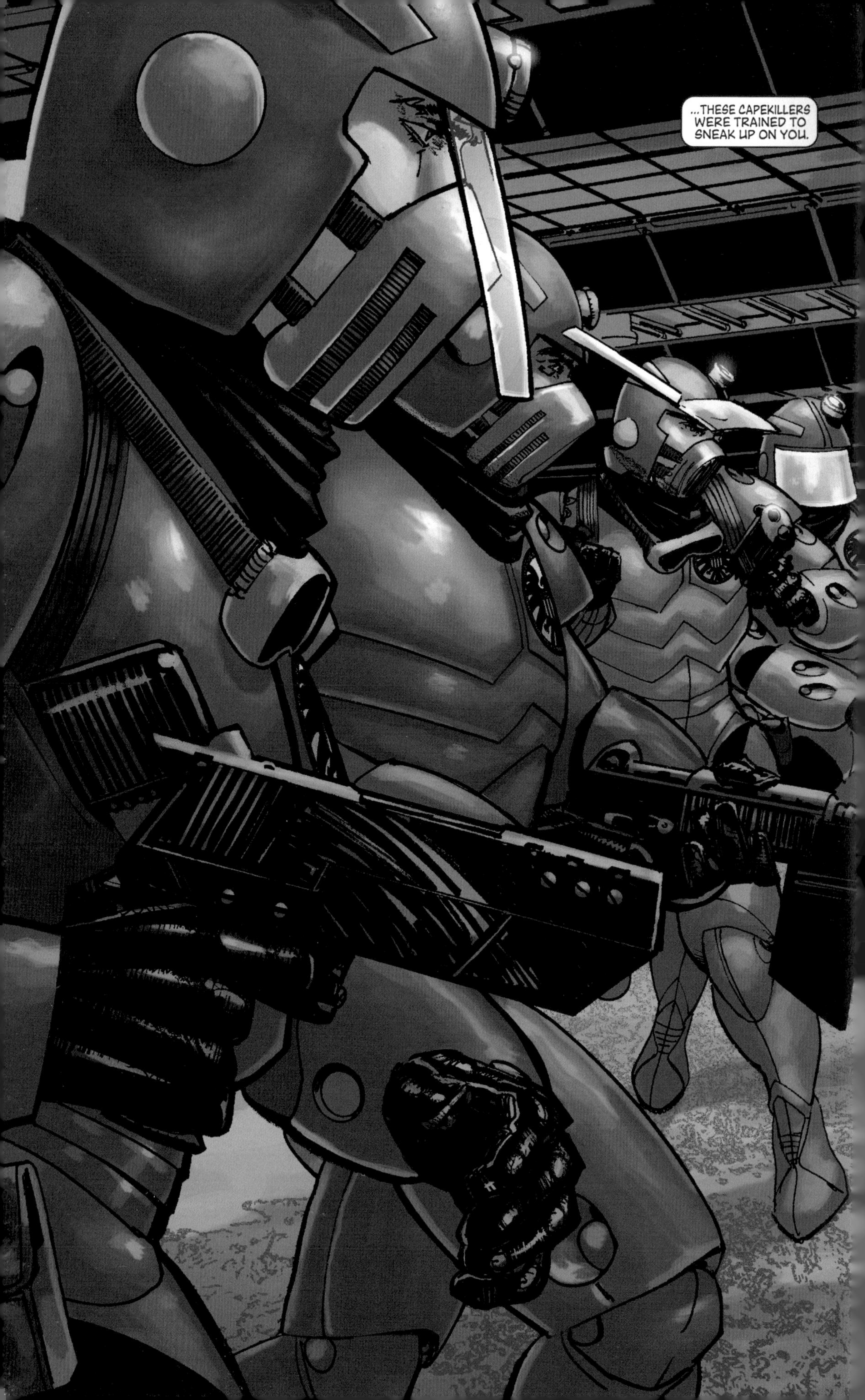
...THESE CAPEKILLERS WERE TRAINED TO SNEAK UP ON YOU.

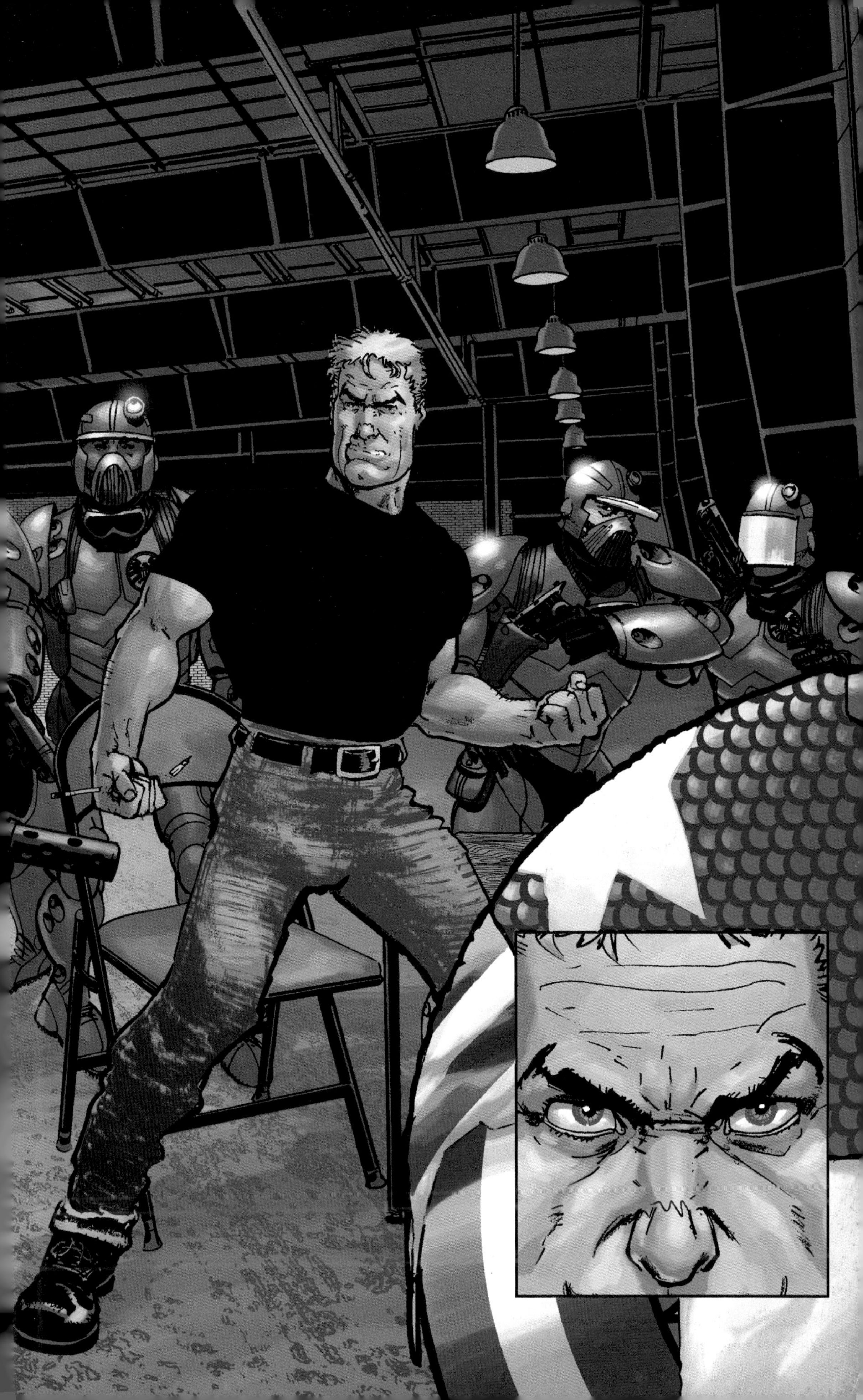

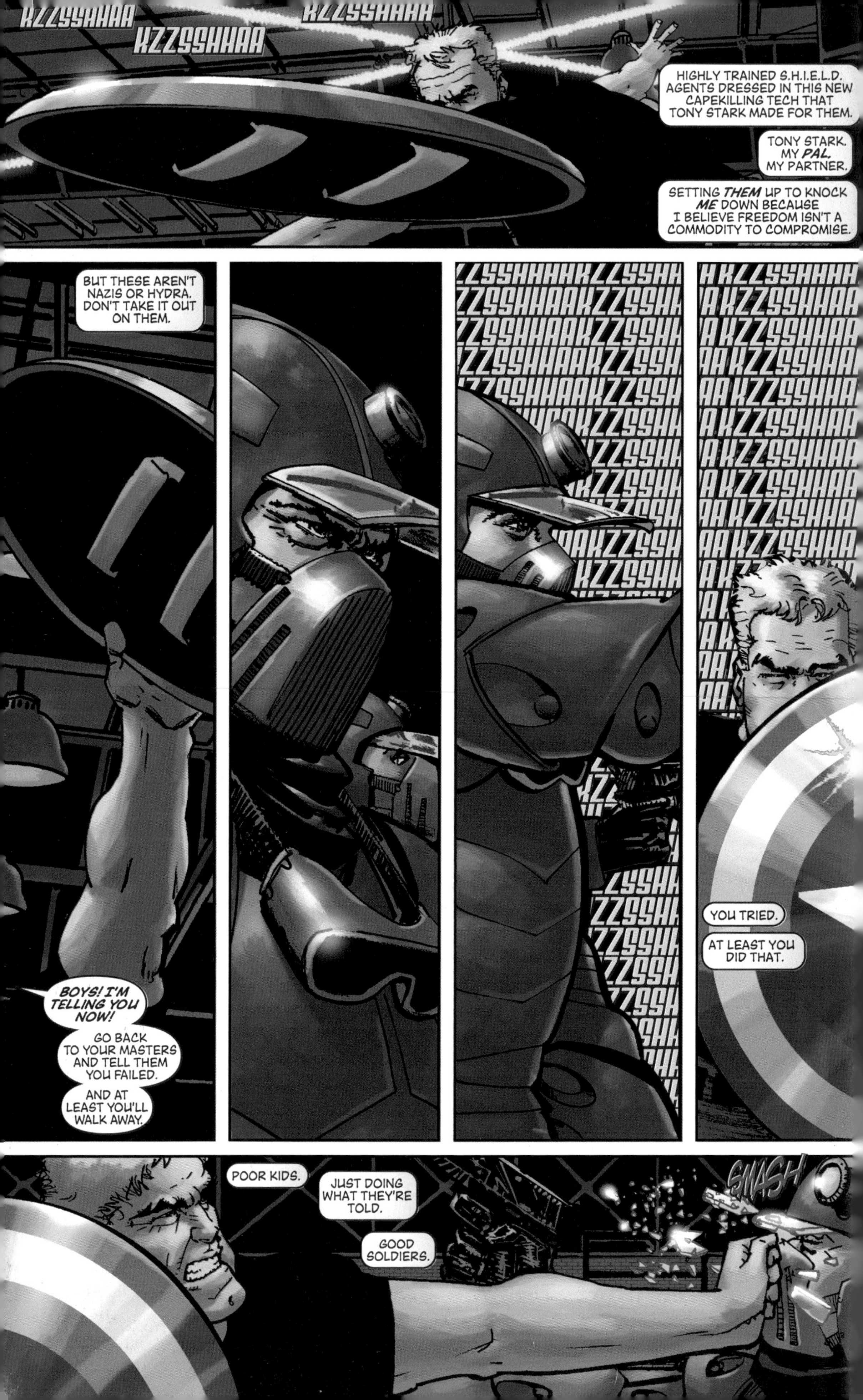
KZZSSHHAA
KZZSSHHAA
KZZSSHHAA
HIGHLY TRAINED S.H.I.E.L.D. AGENTS DRESSED IN THIS NEW CAPEKILLING TECH THAT TONY STARK MADE FOR THEM.
TONY STARK. MY *PAL.* MY PARTNER.
SETTING *THEM* UP TO KNOCK *ME* DOWN BECAUSE I BELIEVE FREEDOM ISN'T A COMMODITY TO COMPROMISE.
BUT THESE AREN'T NAZIS OR HYDRA. DON'T TAKE IT OUT ON THEM.
BOYS! I'M TELLING YOU NOW!
GO BACK TO YOUR MASTERS AND TELL THEM YOU FAILED.
AND AT LEAST YOU'LL WALK AWAY.
YOU TRIED.
AT LEAST YOU DID THAT.
POOR KIDS.
JUST DOING WHAT THEY'RE TOLD.
GOOD SOLDIERS.
SMASH

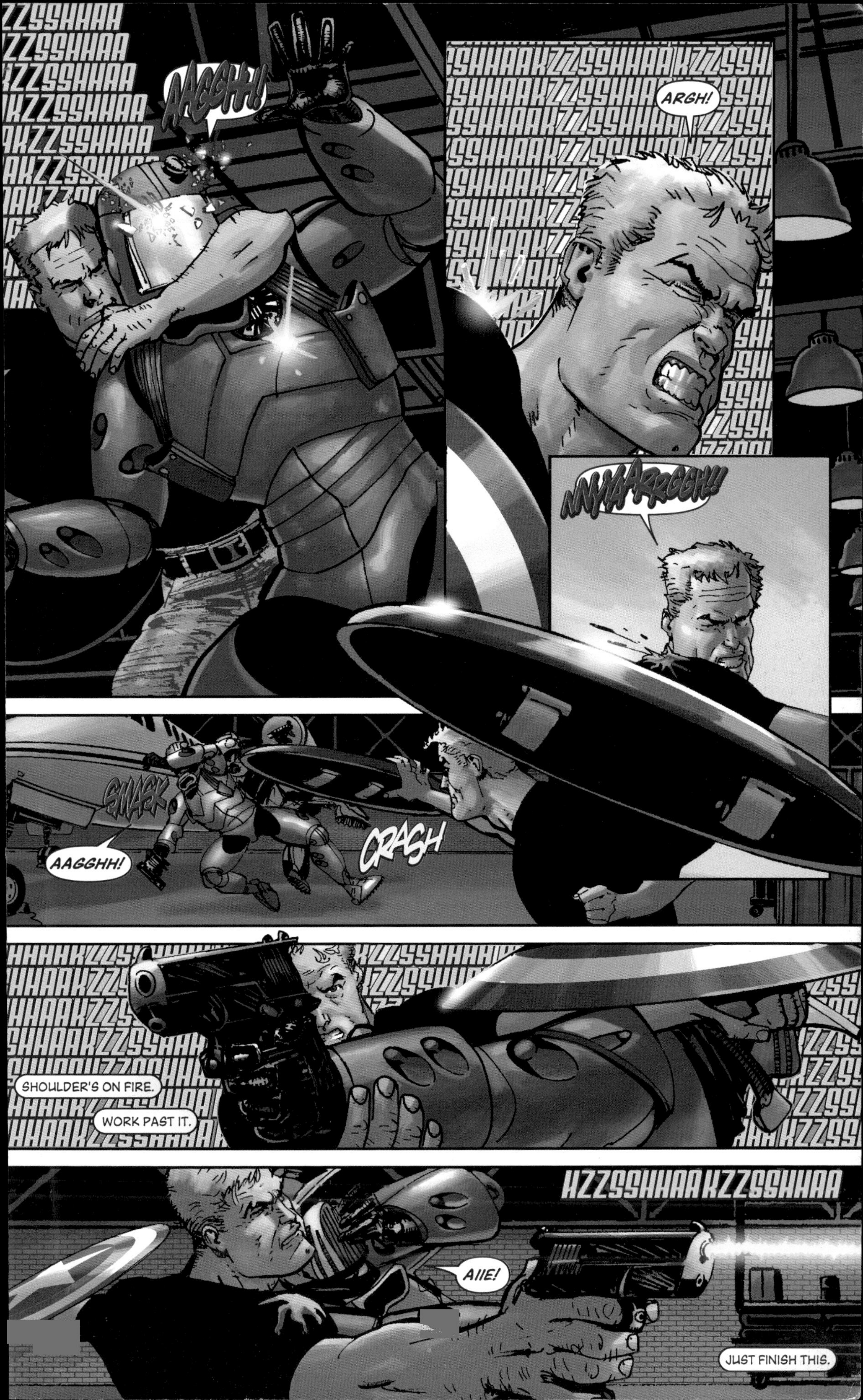
KZZSSHHAA
AAGGHH!
ARGH!
NNYYAARRGGH!!
SMASK
AAGGHH!
CRASH
SHOULDER'S ON FIRE.
WORK PAST IT.
KZZSSHHAA KZZSSHHAA
AIIE!
JUST FINISH THIS.

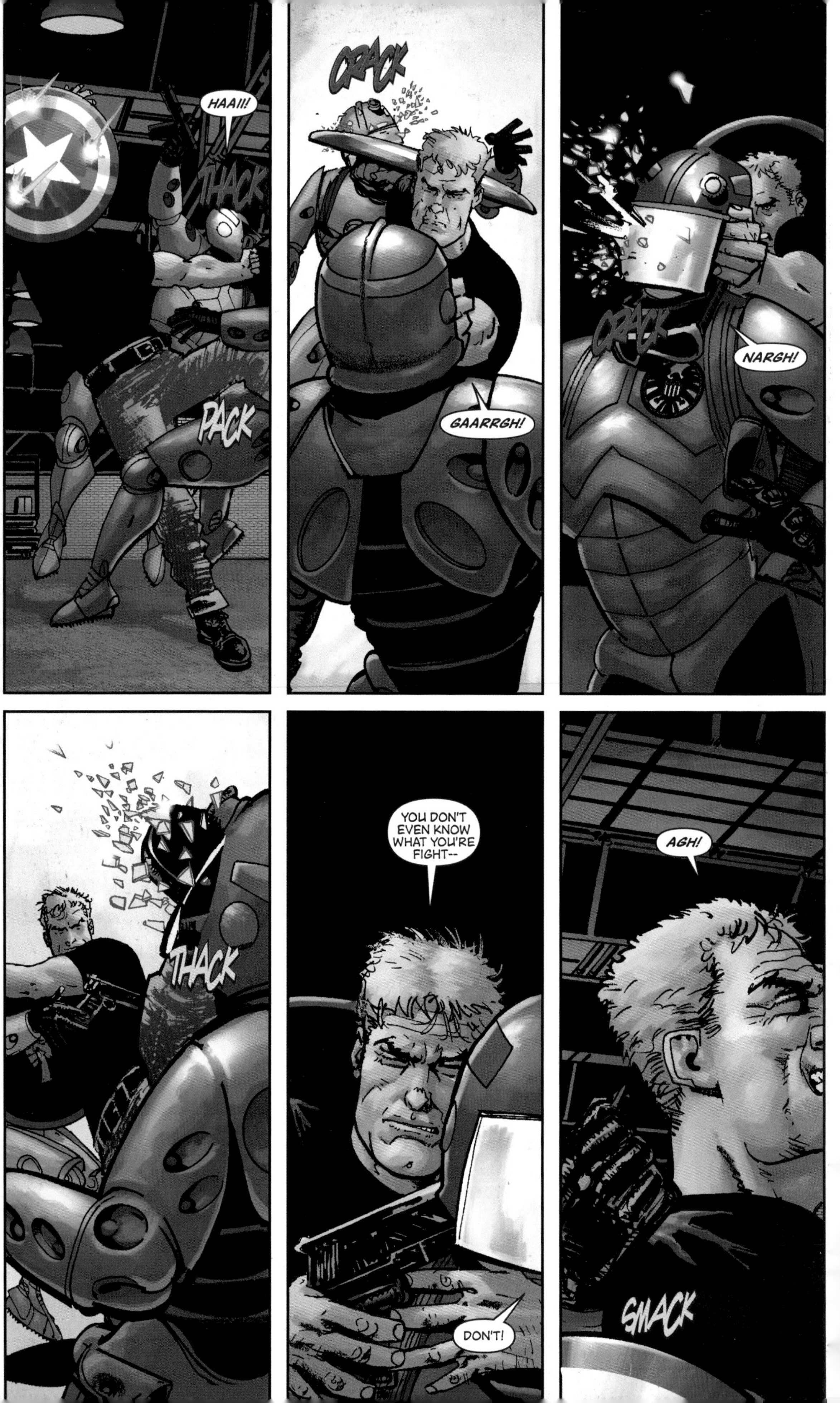
HAAII!
THACK
PACK
CRACK
GAARRGH!
CRACK
NARGH!
THACK
YOU DON'T EVEN KNOW WHAT YOU'RE FIGHT--
DON'T!
AGH!
SMACK

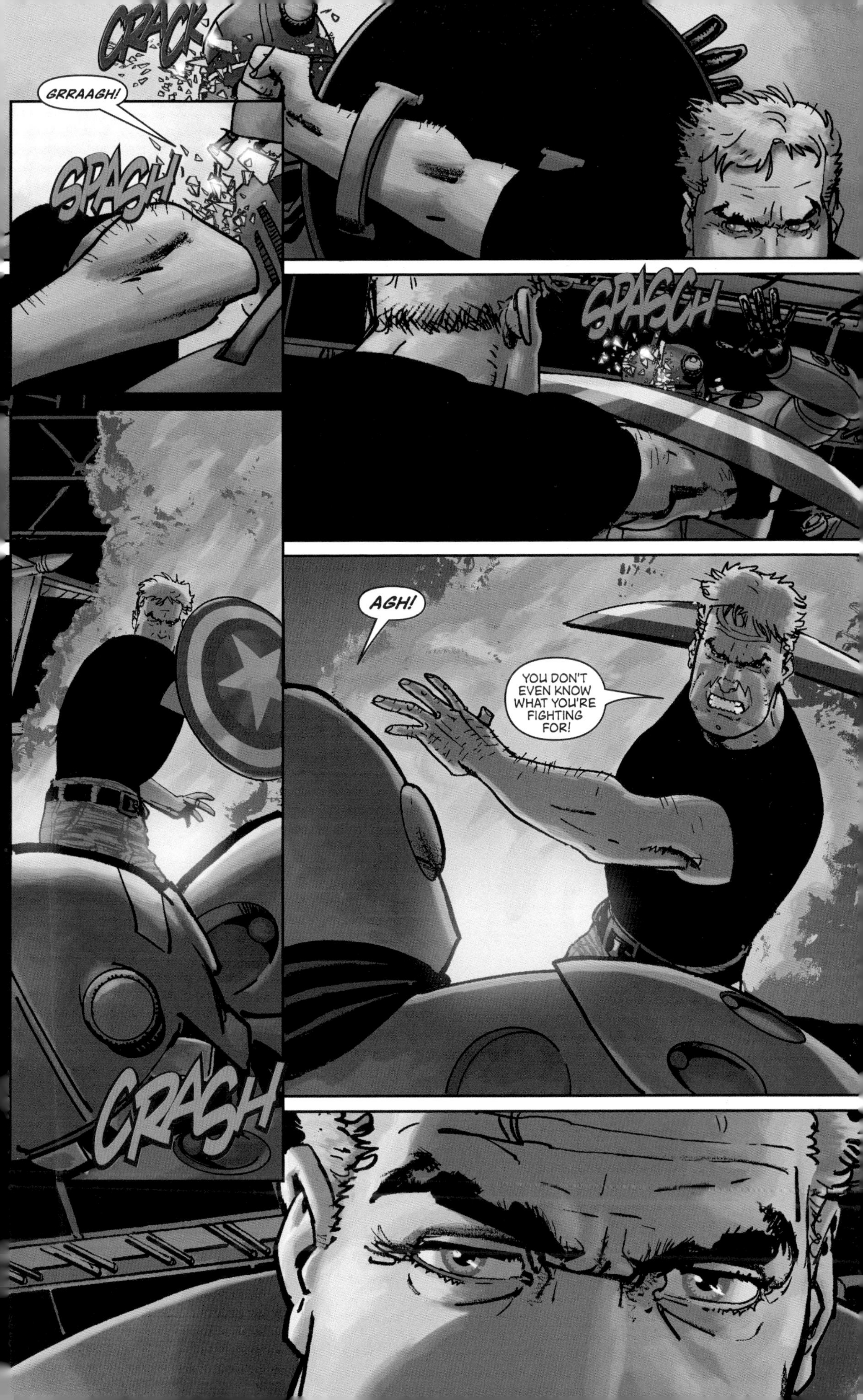
CRACK
GRRAAGH!
SPASH
SPASCH
AGH!
YOU DON'T EVEN KNOW WHAT YOU'RE FIGHTING FOR!
CRASH

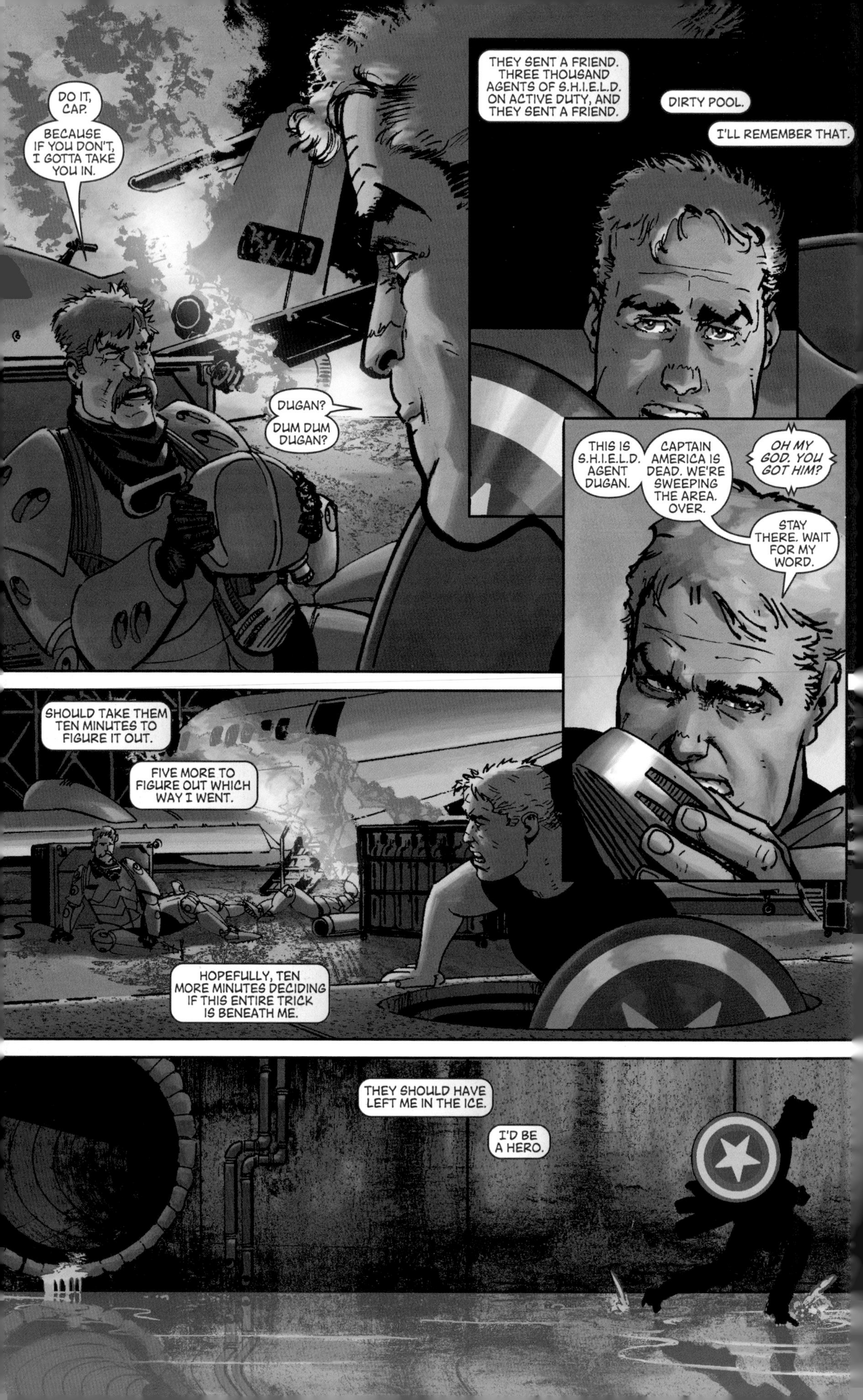
DO IT, CAP.
BECAUSE IF YOU DON'T, I GOTTA TAKE YOU IN.
DUGAN?
DUM DUM DUGAN?
THEY SENT A FRIEND. THREE THOUSAND AGENTS OF S.H.I.E.L.D. ON ACTIVE DUTY, AND THEY SENT A FRIEND.
DIRTY POOL.
I'LL REMEMBER THAT.
THIS IS S.H.I.E.L.D. AGENT DUGAN.
CAPTAIN AMERICA IS DEAD. WE'RE SWEEPING THE AREA. OVER.
OH MY GOD. YOU GOT HIM?
STAY THERE. WAIT FOR MY WORD.
SHOULD TAKE THEM TEN MINUTES TO FIGURE IT OUT.
FIVE MORE TO FIGURE OUT WHICH WAY I WENT.
HOPEFULLY, TEN MORE MINUTES DECIDING IF THIS ENTIRE TRICK IS BENEATH ME.
THEY SHOULD HAVE LEFT ME IN THE ICE.
I'D BE A HERO.

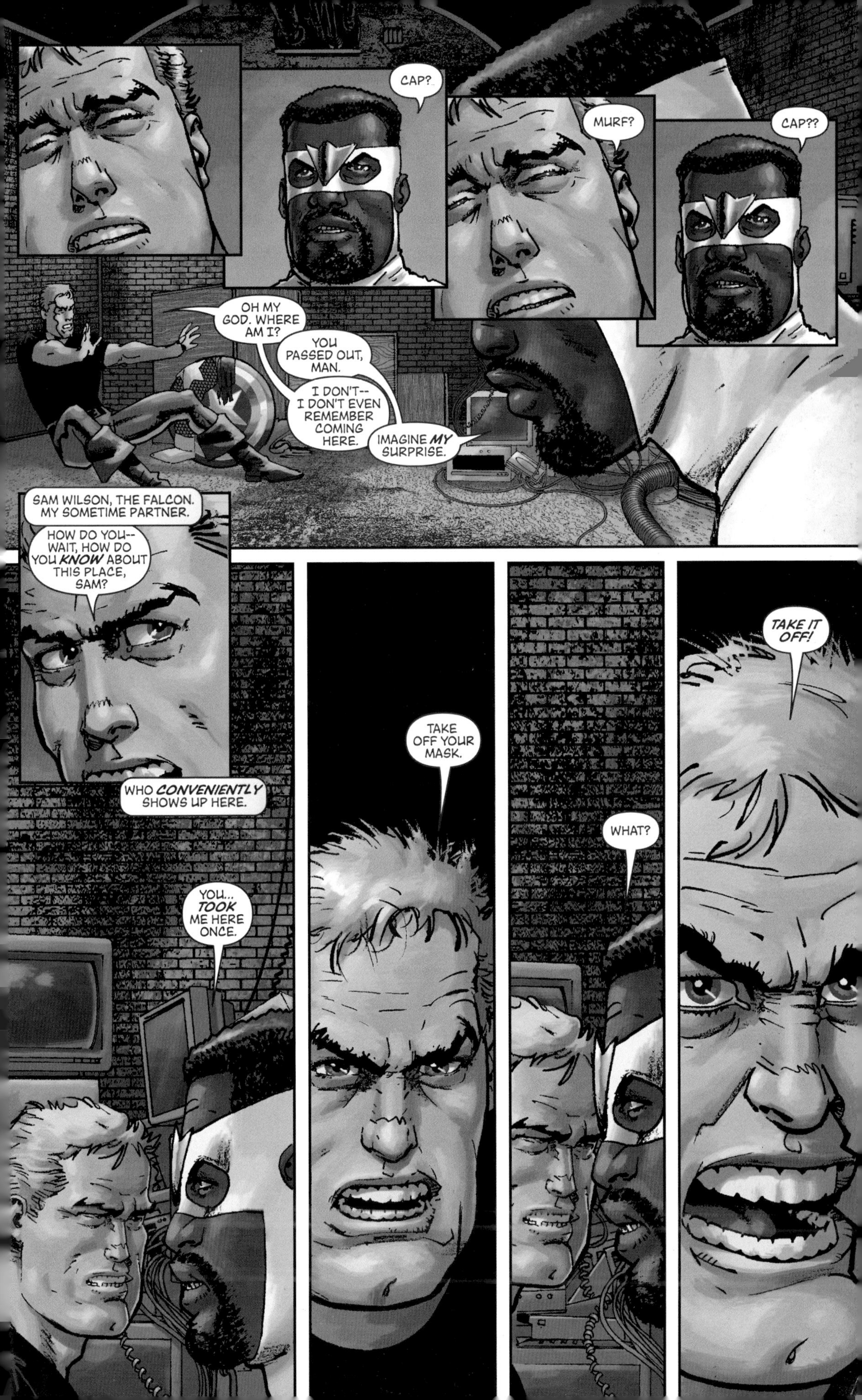
CAP?
MURF?
CAP??
OH MY GOD. WHERE AM I?
YOU PASSED OUT, MAN.
I DON'T-- I DON'T EVEN REMEMBER COMING HERE.
IMAGINE MY SURPRISE.
SAM WILSON, THE FALCON. MY SOMETIME PARTNER.
HOW DO YOU-- WAIT, HOW DO YOU KNOW ABOUT THIS PLACE, SAM?
WHO CONVENIENTLY SHOWS UP HERE.
YOU... TOOK ME HERE ONCE.
TAKE OFF YOUR MASK.
WHAT?
TAKE IT OFF!

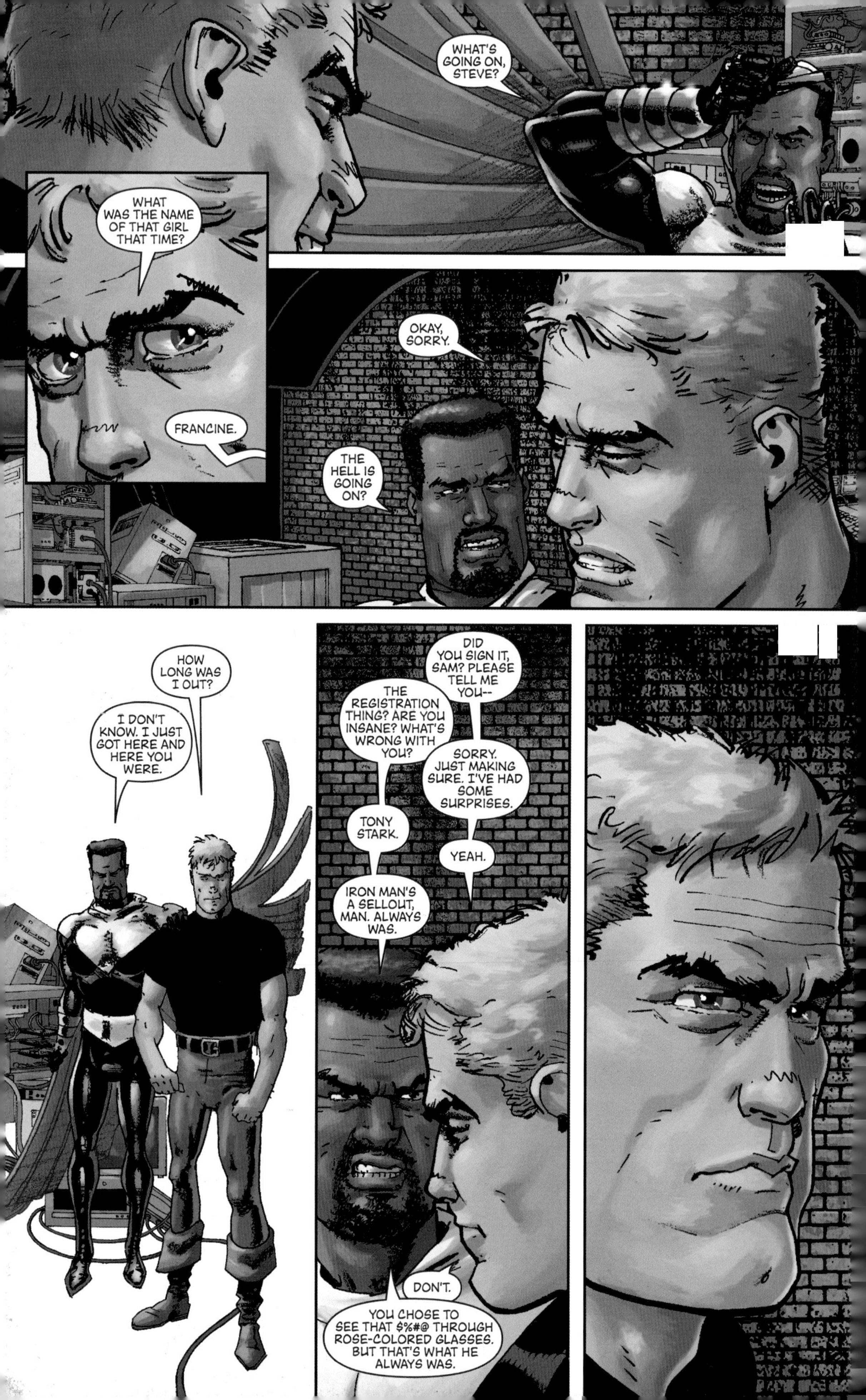
WHAT'S GOING ON, STEVE?
WHAT WAS THE NAME OF THAT GIRL THAT TIME?
FRANCINE.
OKAY, SORRY.
THE HELL IS GOING ON?
HOW LONG WAS I OUT?
I DON'T KNOW. I JUST GOT HERE AND HERE YOU WERE.
DID YOU SIGN IT, SAM? PLEASE TELL ME YOU--
THE REGISTRATION THING? ARE YOU INSANE? WHAT'S WRONG WITH YOU?
SORRY. JUST MAKING SURE. I'VE HAD SOME SURPRISES.
TONY STARK.
YEAH.
IRON MAN'S A SELLOUT, MAN. ALWAYS WAS.
DON'T.
YOU CHOSE TO SEE THAT $%#@ THROUGH ROSE-COLORED GLASSES. BUT THAT'S WHAT HE ALWAYS WAS.

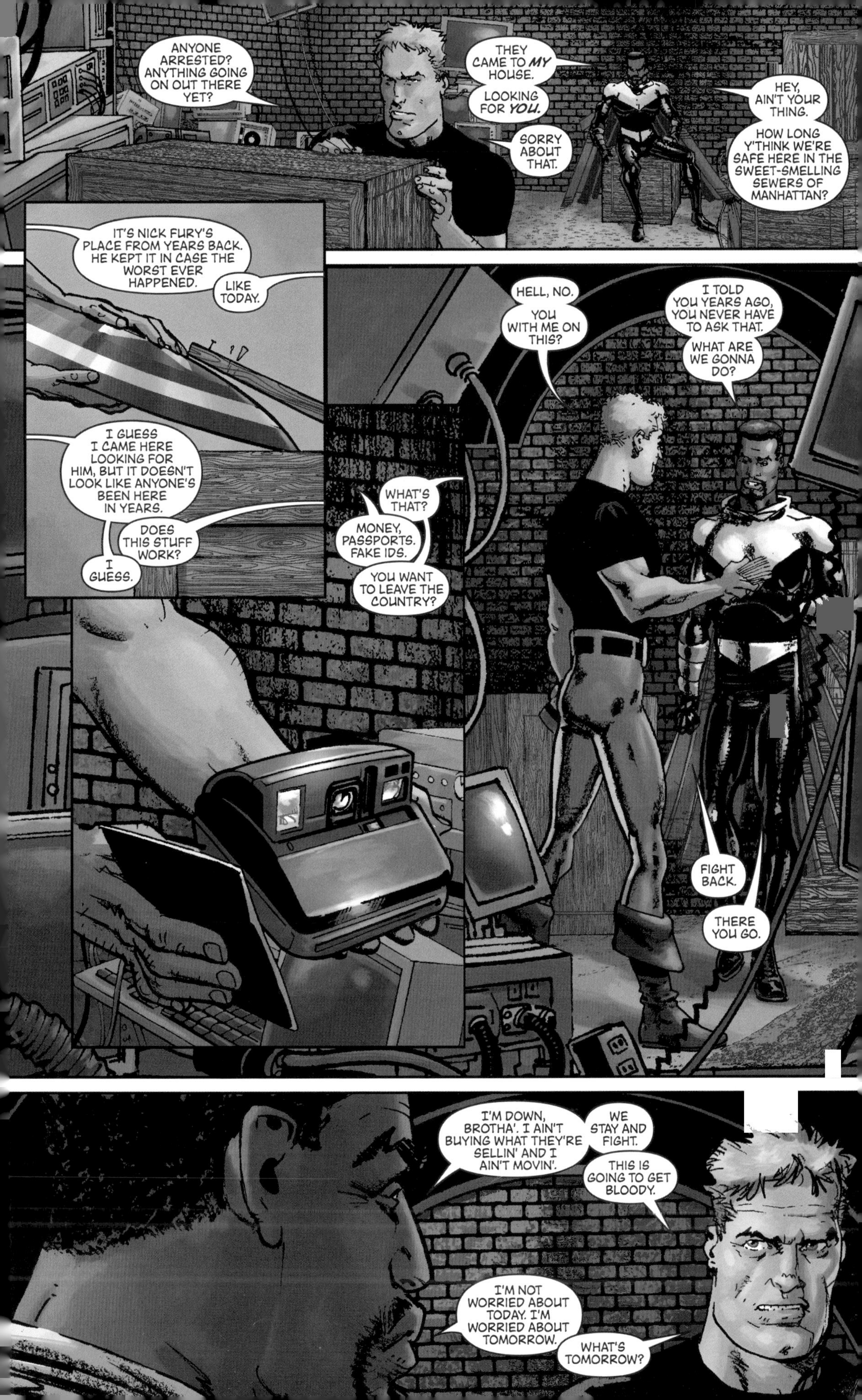
ANYONE ARRESTED? ANYTHING GOING ON OUT THERE YET?
THEY CAME TO *MY* HOUSE.
LOOKING FOR *YOU.*
SORRY ABOUT THAT.
HEY, AIN'T YOUR THING.
HOW LONG Y'THINK WE'RE SAFE HERE IN THE SWEET-SMELLING SEWERS OF MANHATTAN?
IT'S NICK FURY'S PLACE FROM YEARS BACK. HE KEPT IT IN CASE THE WORST EVER HAPPENED.
LIKE TODAY.
I GUESS I CAME HERE LOOKING FOR HIM, BUT IT DOESN'T LOOK LIKE ANYONE'S BEEN HERE IN YEARS.
DOES THIS STUFF WORK?
I GUESS.
WHAT'S THAT?
MONEY, PASSPORTS. FAKE IDS.
YOU WANT TO LEAVE THE COUNTRY?
HELL, NO.
YOU WITH ME ON THIS?
I TOLD YOU YEARS AGO, YOU NEVER HAVE TO ASK THAT.
WHAT ARE WE GONNA DO?
FIGHT BACK.
THERE YOU GO.
I'M DOWN, BROTHA'. I AIN'T BUYING WHAT THEY'RE SELLIN' AND I AIN'T MOVIN'.
WE STAY AND FIGHT.
THIS IS GOING TO GET BLOODY.
I'M NOT WORRIED ABOUT TODAY. I'M WORRIED ABOUT TOMORROW.
WHAT'S TOMORROW?

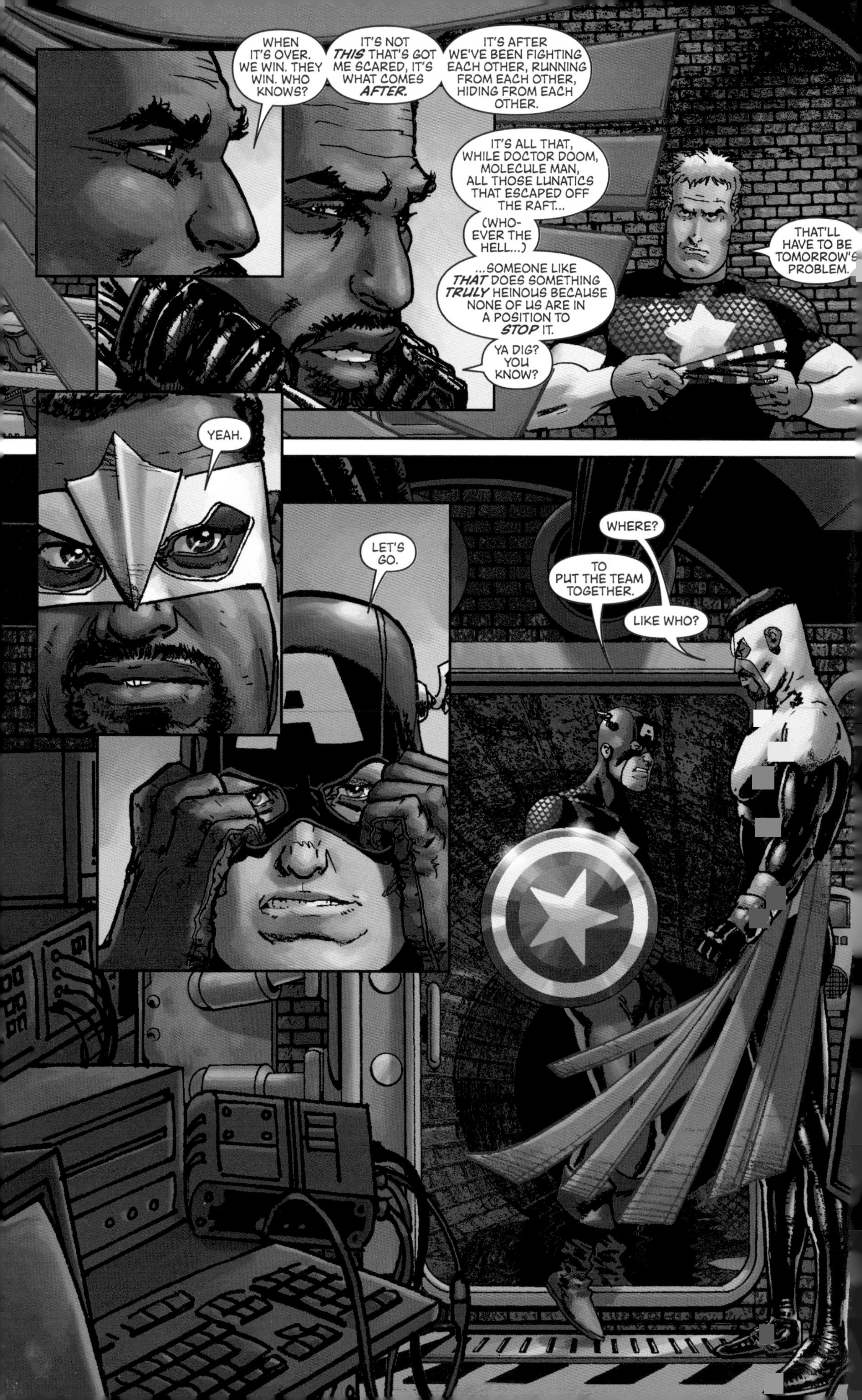

WHEN IT'S OVER. WE WIN. THEY WIN. WHO KNOWS?
IT'S NOT THIS THAT'S GOT ME SCARED, IT'S WHAT COMES AFTER.
IT'S AFTER WE'VE BEEN FIGHTING EACH OTHER, RUNNING FROM EACH OTHER, HIDING FROM EACH OTHER.
IT'S ALL THAT, WHILE DOCTOR DOOM, MOLECULE MAN, ALL THOSE LUNATICS THAT ESCAPED OFF THE RAFT...
(WHO-EVER THE HELL...)
...SOMEONE LIKE THAT DOES SOMETHING TRULY HEINOUS BECAUSE NONE OF US ARE IN A POSITION TO STOP IT.
YA DIG? YOU KNOW?
THAT'LL HAVE TO BE TOMORROW'S PROBLEM.
YEAH.
LET'S GO.
WHERE?
TO PUT THE TEAM TOGETHER.
LIKE WHO?

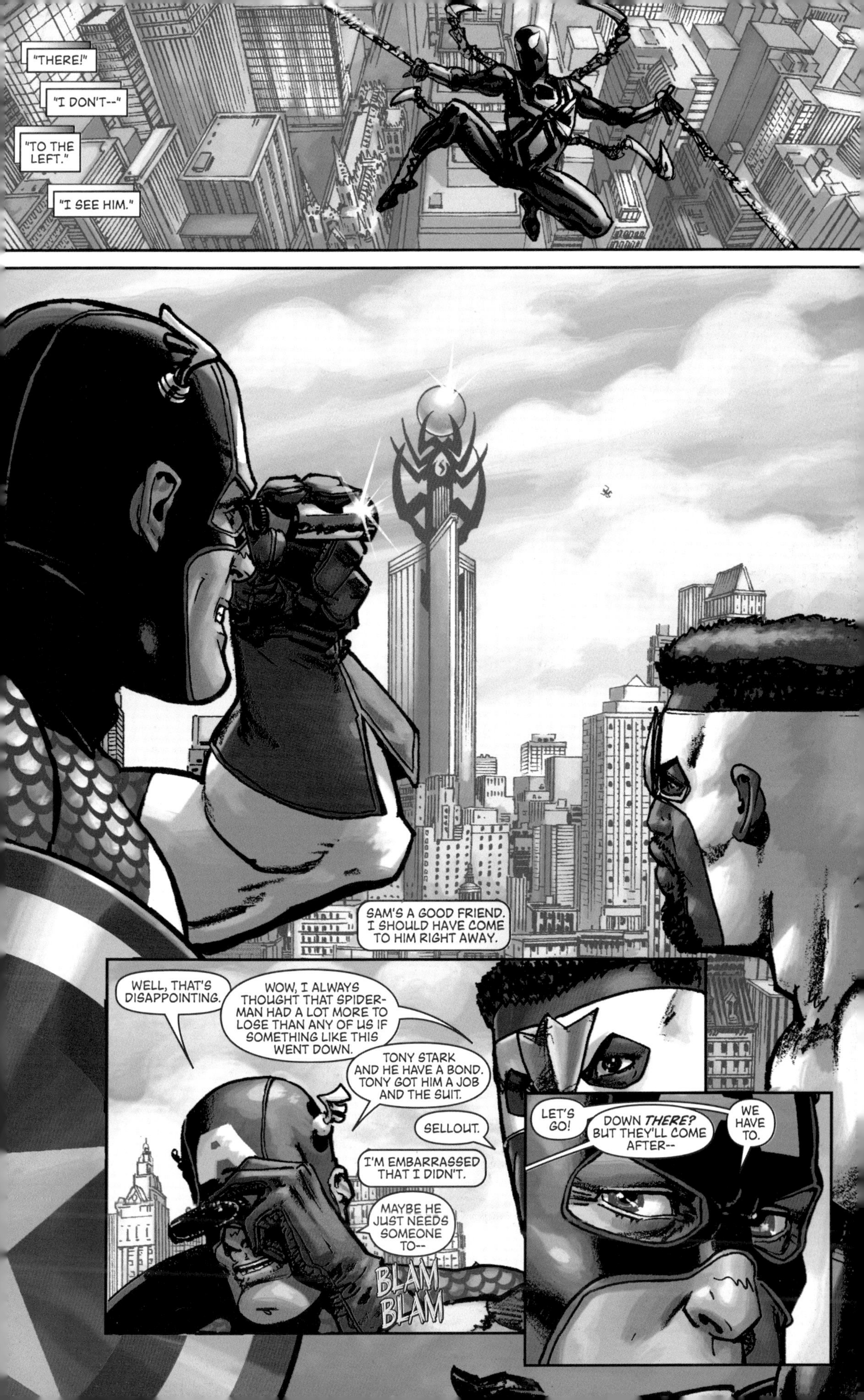
"THERE!"
"I DON'T--"
"TO THE LEFT."
"I SEE HIM."
SAM'S A GOOD FRIEND. I SHOULD HAVE COME TO HIM RIGHT AWAY.
WELL, THAT'S DISAPPOINTING.
WOW, I ALWAYS THOUGHT THAT SPIDER-MAN HAD A LOT MORE TO LOSE THAN ANY OF US IF SOMETHING LIKE THIS WENT DOWN.
TONY STARK AND HE HAVE A BOND. TONY GOT HIM A JOB AND THE SUIT.
SELLOUT.
I'M EMBARRASSED THAT I DIDN'T.
MAYBE HE JUST NEEDS SOMEONE TO--
BLAM BLAM
LET'S GO!
DOWN *THERE?* BUT THEY'LL COME AFTER--
WE HAVE TO.

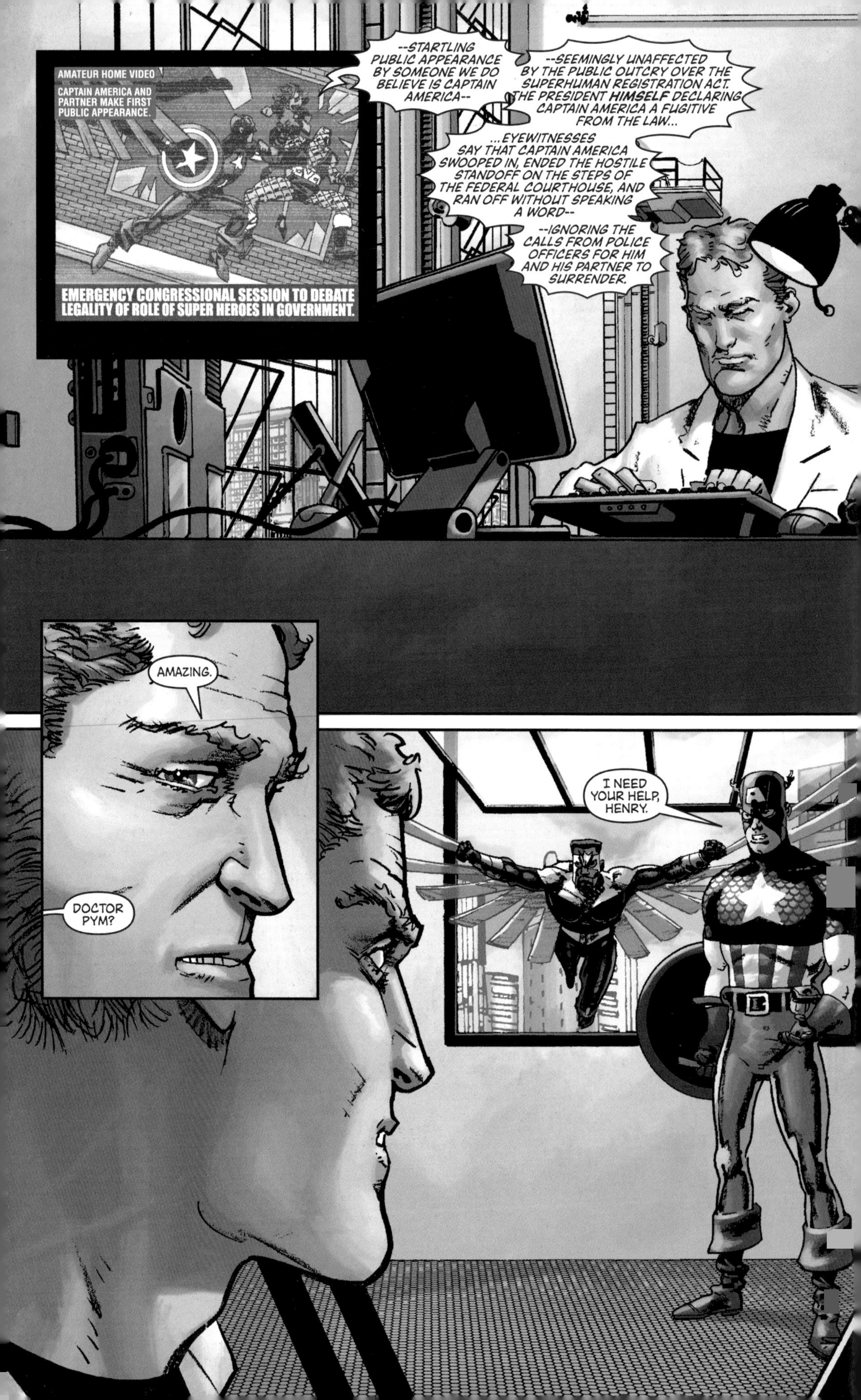
AMATEUR HOME VIDEO
CAPTAIN AMERICA AND PARTNER MAKE FIRST PUBLIC APPEARANCE.
EMERGENCY CONGRESSIONAL SESSION TO DEBATE LEGALITY OF ROLE OF SUPER HEROES IN GOVERNMENT.
--STARTLING PUBLIC APPEARANCE BY SOMEONE WE DO BELIEVE IS CAPTAIN AMERICA--
--SEEMINGLY UNAFFECTED BY THE PUBLIC OUTCRY OVER THE SUPERHUMAN REGISTRATION ACT. THE PRESIDENT HIMSELF DECLARING CAPTAIN AMERICA A FUGITIVE FROM THE LAW...
...EYEWITNESSES SAY THAT CAPTAIN AMERICA SWOOPED IN, ENDED THE HOSTILE STANDOFF ON THE STEPS OF THE FEDERAL COURTHOUSE, AND RAN OFF WITHOUT SPEAKING A WORD--
--IGNORING THE CALLS FROM POLICE OFFICERS FOR HIM AND HIS PARTNER TO SURRENDER.
AMAZING.
DOCTOR PYM?
I NEED YOUR HELP, HENRY.

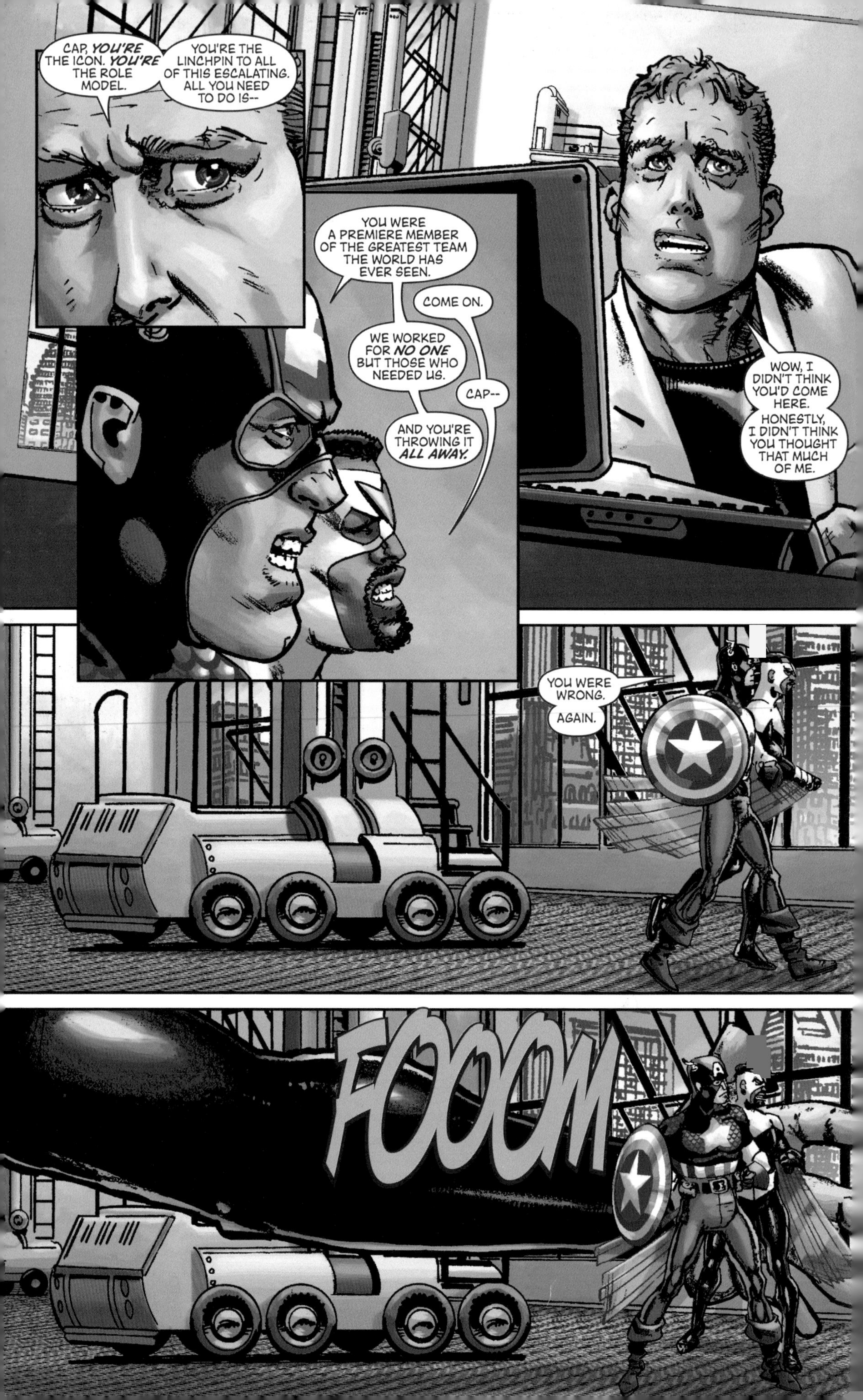
CAP, *YOU'RE* THE ICON. *YOU'RE* THE ROLE MODEL.
YOU'RE THE LINCHPIN TO ALL OF THIS ESCALATING. ALL YOU NEED TO DO IS--
YOU WERE A PREMIERE MEMBER OF THE GREATEST TEAM THE WORLD HAS EVER SEEN.
COME ON.
WE WORKED FOR *NO ONE* BUT THOSE WHO NEEDED US.
CAP--
AND YOU'RE THROWING IT *ALL AWAY.*
WOW, I DIDN'T THINK YOU'D COME HERE.
HONESTLY, I DIDN'T THINK YOU THOUGHT THAT MUCH OF ME.
YOU WERE WRONG.
AGAIN.
FOOOM

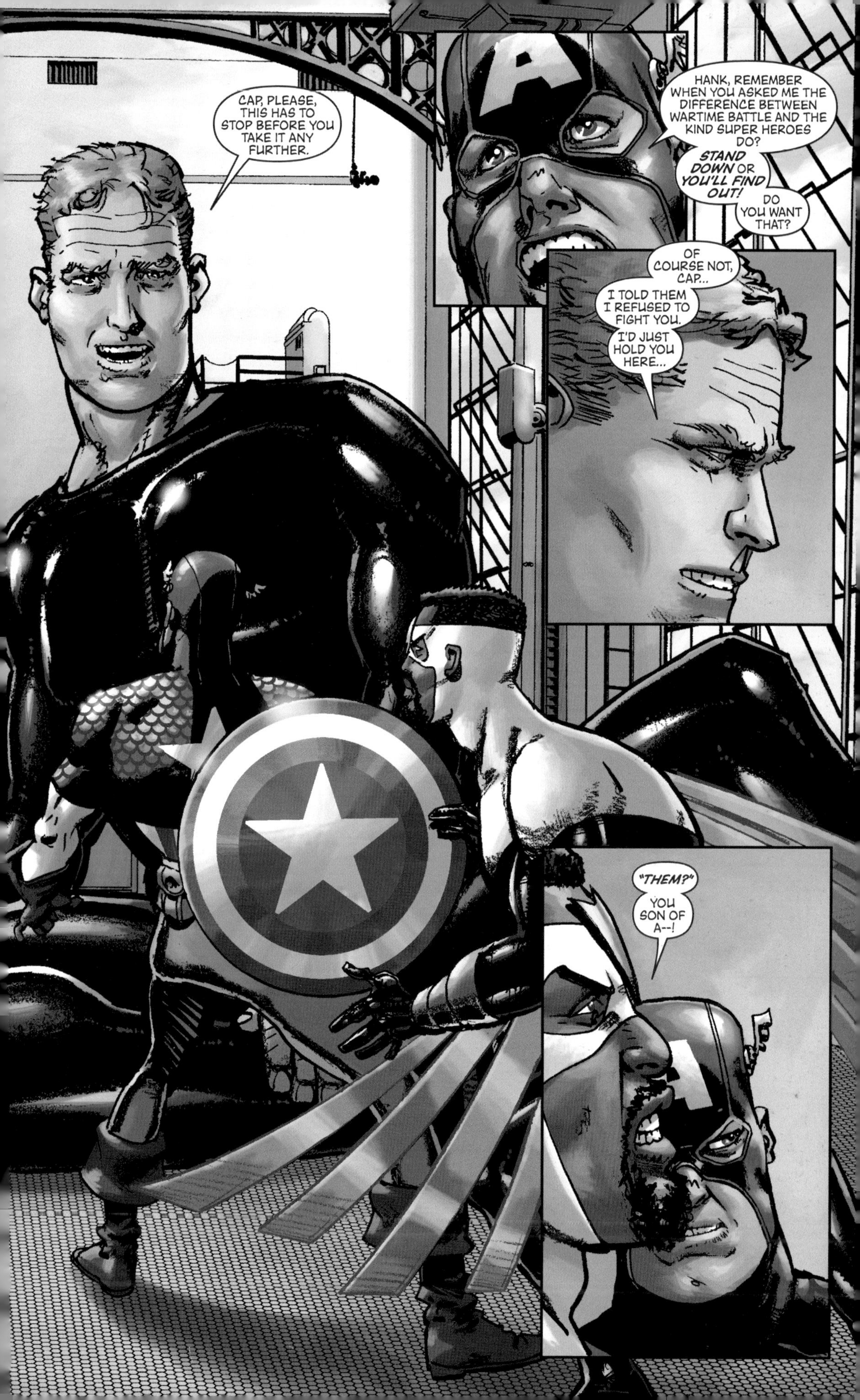
CAP, PLEASE, THIS HAS TO STOP BEFORE YOU TAKE IT ANY FURTHER.
HANK, REMEMBER WHEN YOU ASKED ME THE DIFFERENCE BETWEEN WARTIME BATTLE AND THE KIND SUPER HEROES DO?
STAND DOWN OR YOU'LL FIND OUT!
DO YOU WANT THAT?
OF COURSE NOT, CAP...
I TOLD THEM I REFUSED TO FIGHT YOU.
I'D JUST HOLD YOU HERE...
"THEM?"
YOU SON OF A--!

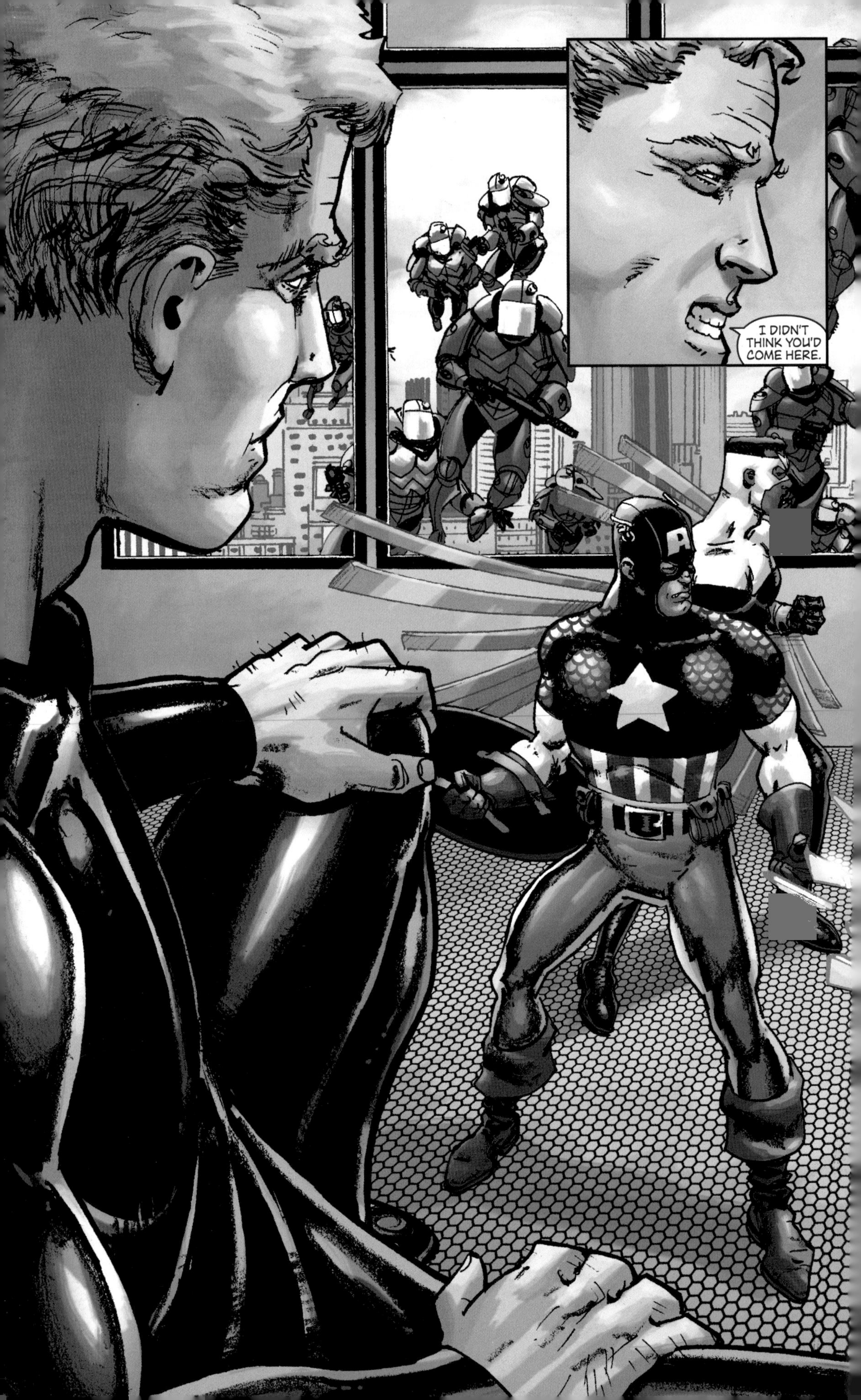
I DIDN'T THINK YOU'D COME HERE.

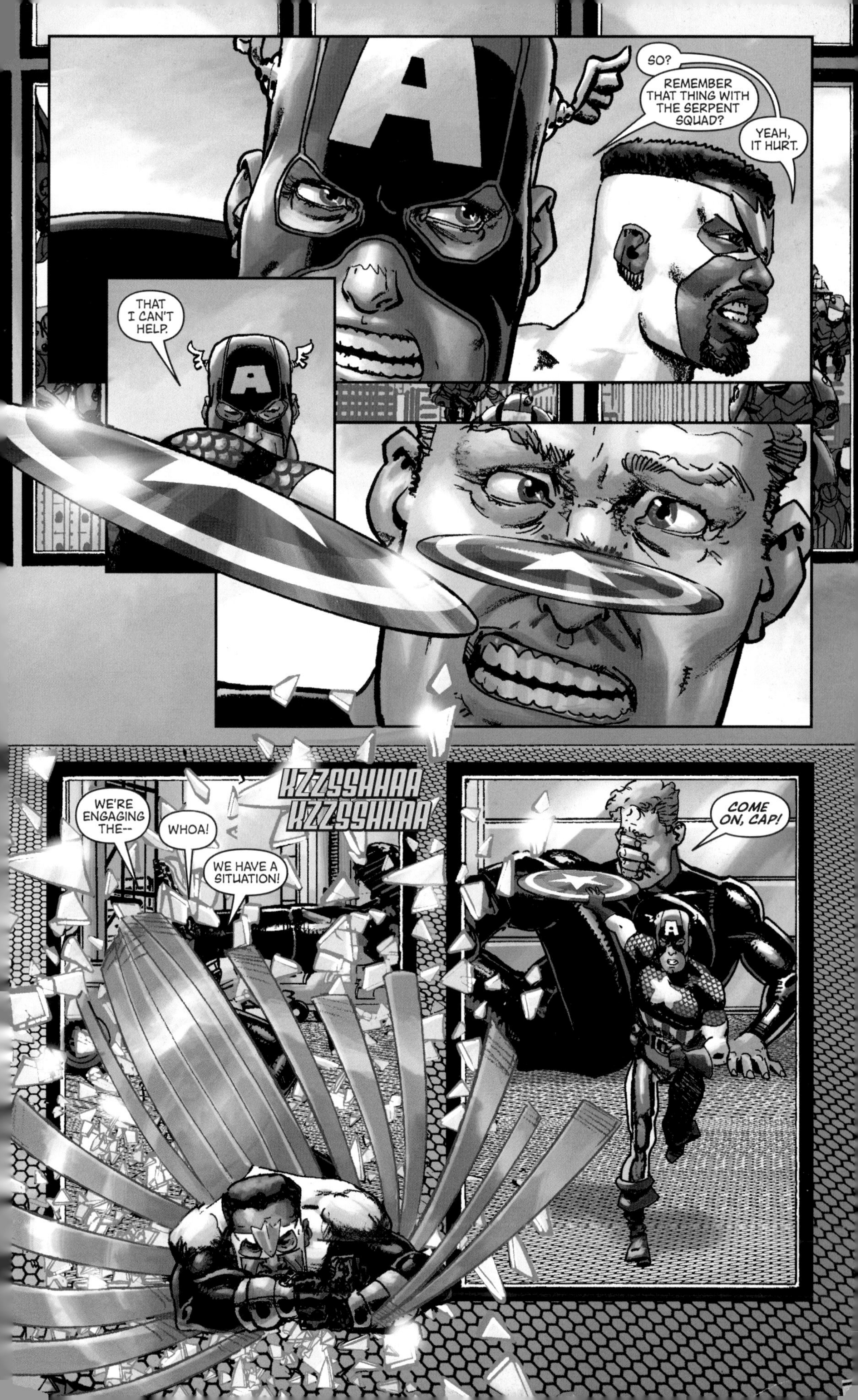
SO?
REMEMBER THAT THING WITH THE SERPENT SQUAD?
YEAH, IT HURT.
THAT I CAN'T HELP.
KZZSSHHAA KZZSSHHAA
WE'RE ENGAGING THE--
WHOA!
WE HAVE A SITUATION!
COME ON, CAP!

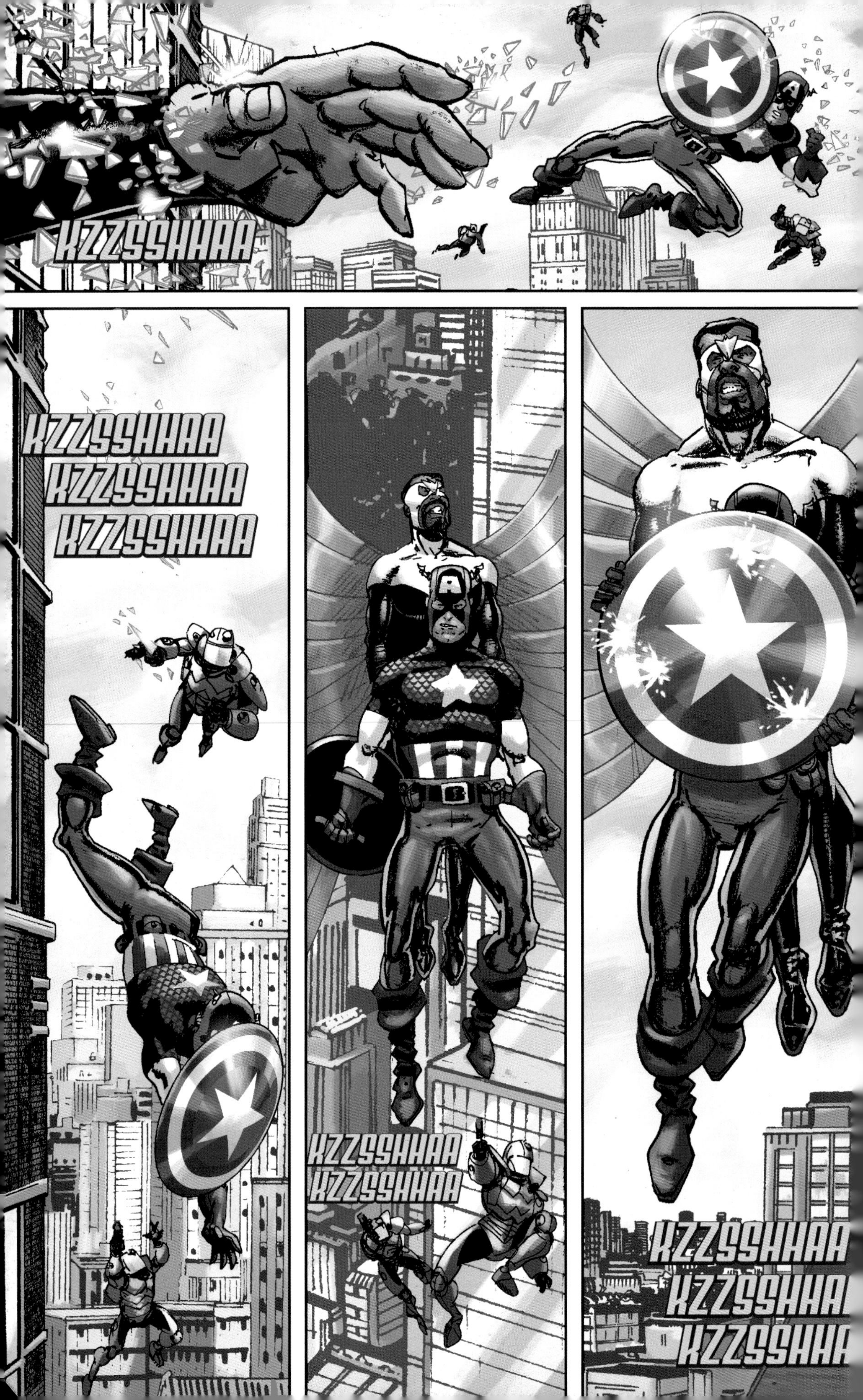
KZZSSHHAA
KZZSSHHAA
KZZSSHHAA
KZZSSHHAA
KZZSSHHAA
KZZSSHHAA
KZZSSHHAA
KZZSSHHA
KZZSSHH

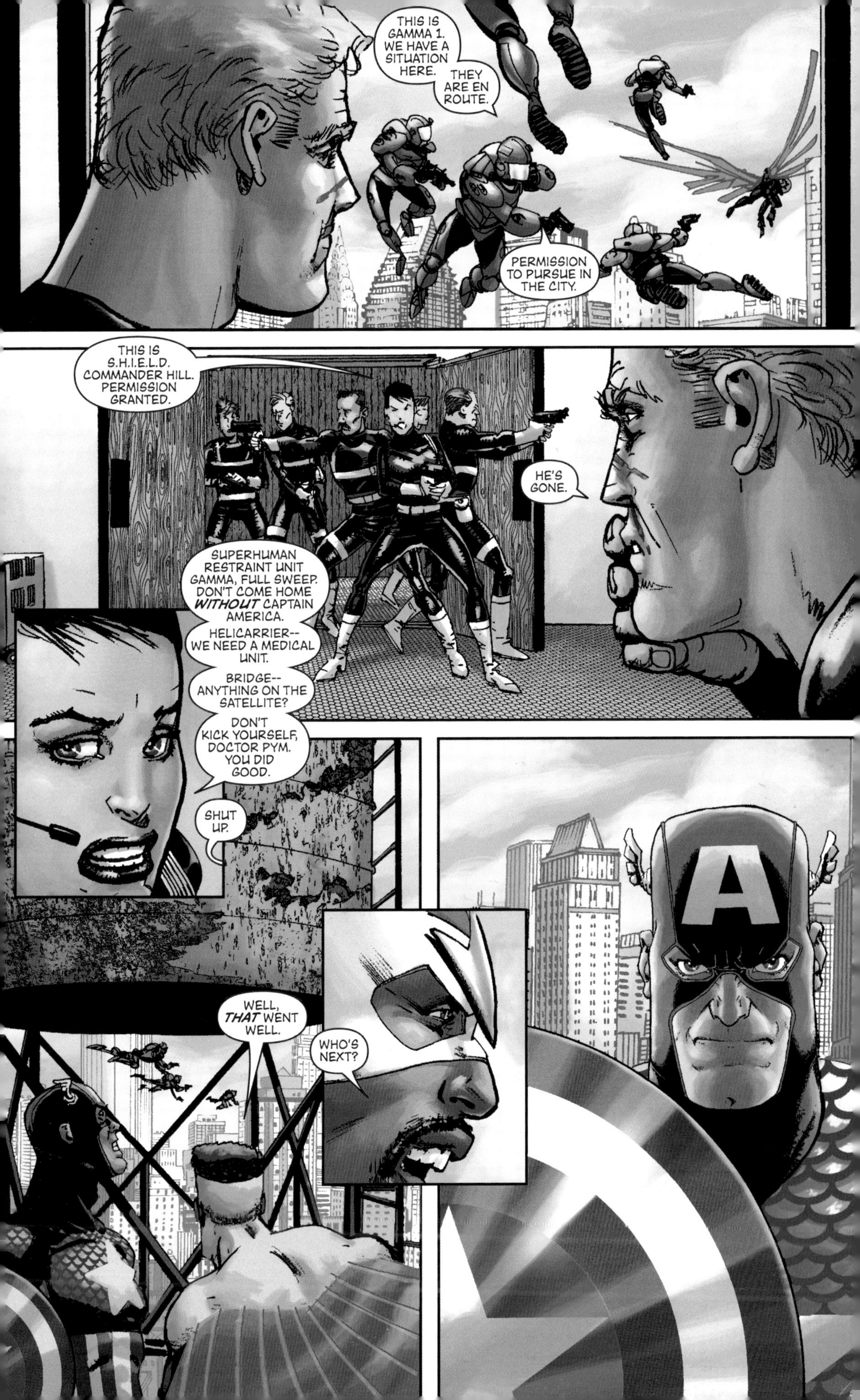
THIS IS GAMMA 1. WE HAVE A SITUATION HERE.
THEY ARE EN ROUTE.
PERMISSION TO PURSUE IN THE CITY.
THIS IS S.H.I.E.L.D. COMMANDER HILL. PERMISSION GRANTED.
HE'S GONE.
SUPERHUMAN RESTRAINT UNIT GAMMA, FULL SWEEP. DON'T COME HOME *WITHOUT* CAPTAIN AMERICA.
HELICARRIER-- WE NEED A MEDICAL UNIT.
BRIDGE-- ANYTHING ON THE SATELLITE?
DON'T KICK YOURSELF, DOCTOR PYM. YOU DID GOOD.
SHUT UP.
WELL, *THAT* WENT WELL.
WHO'S NEXT?

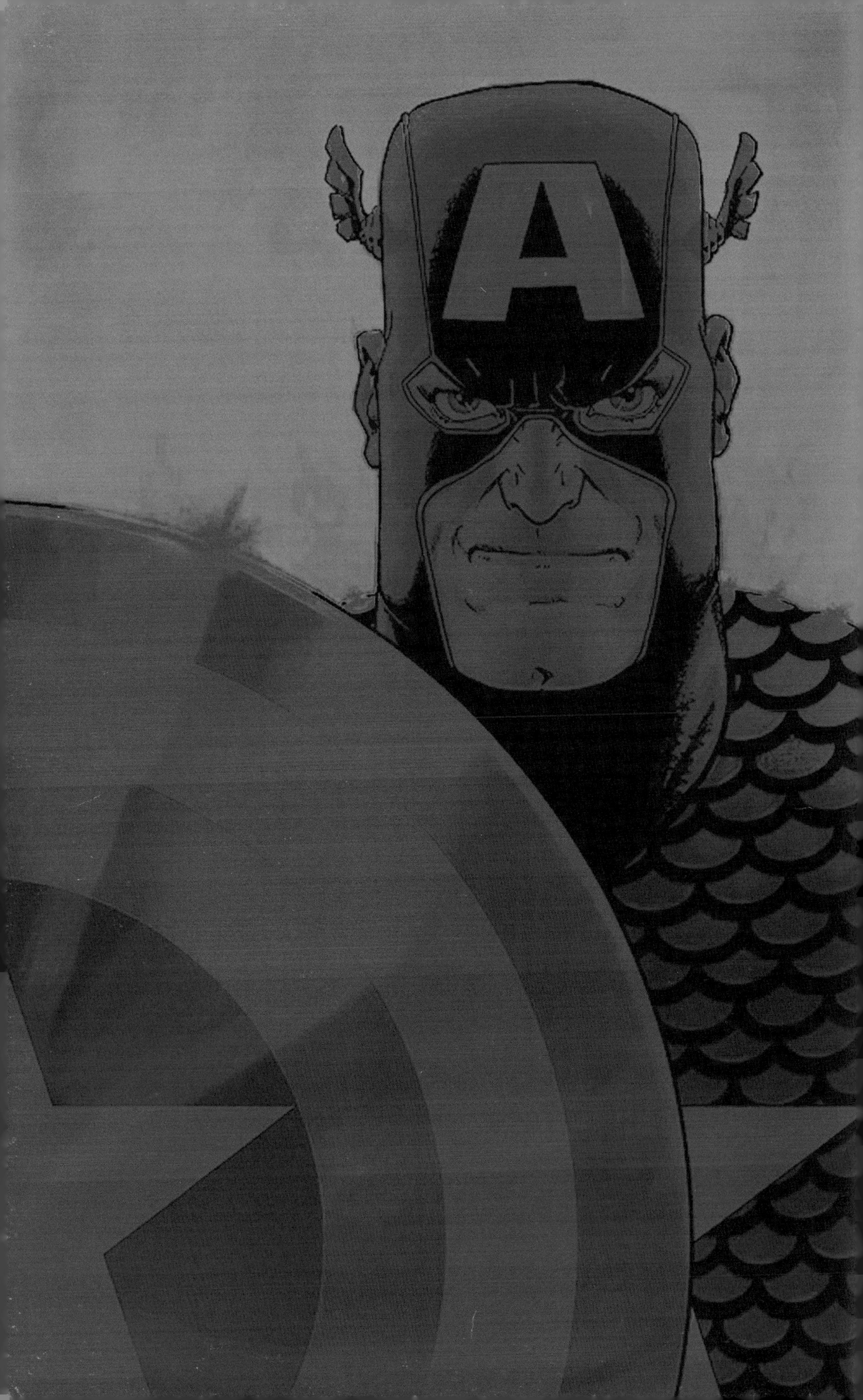

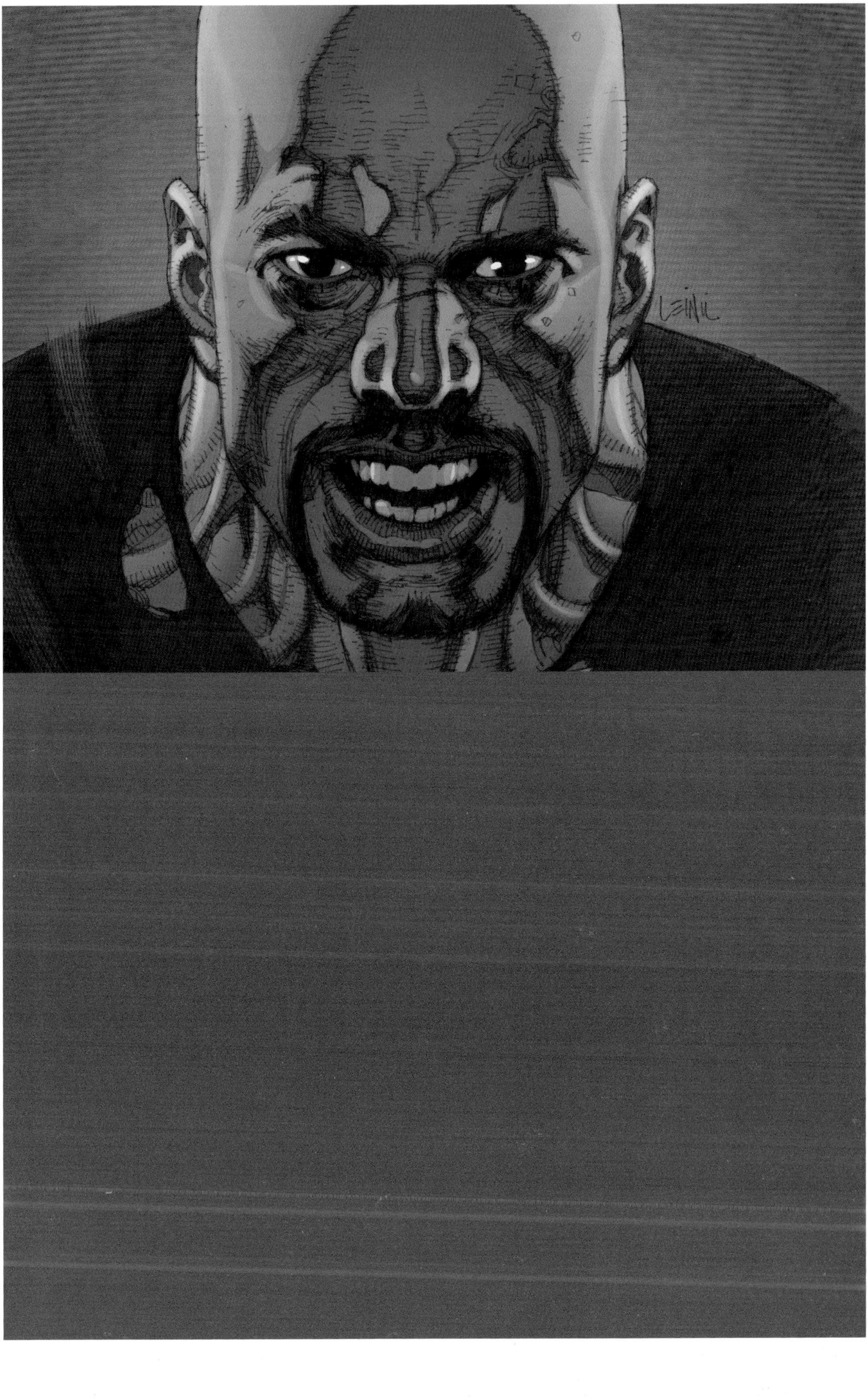

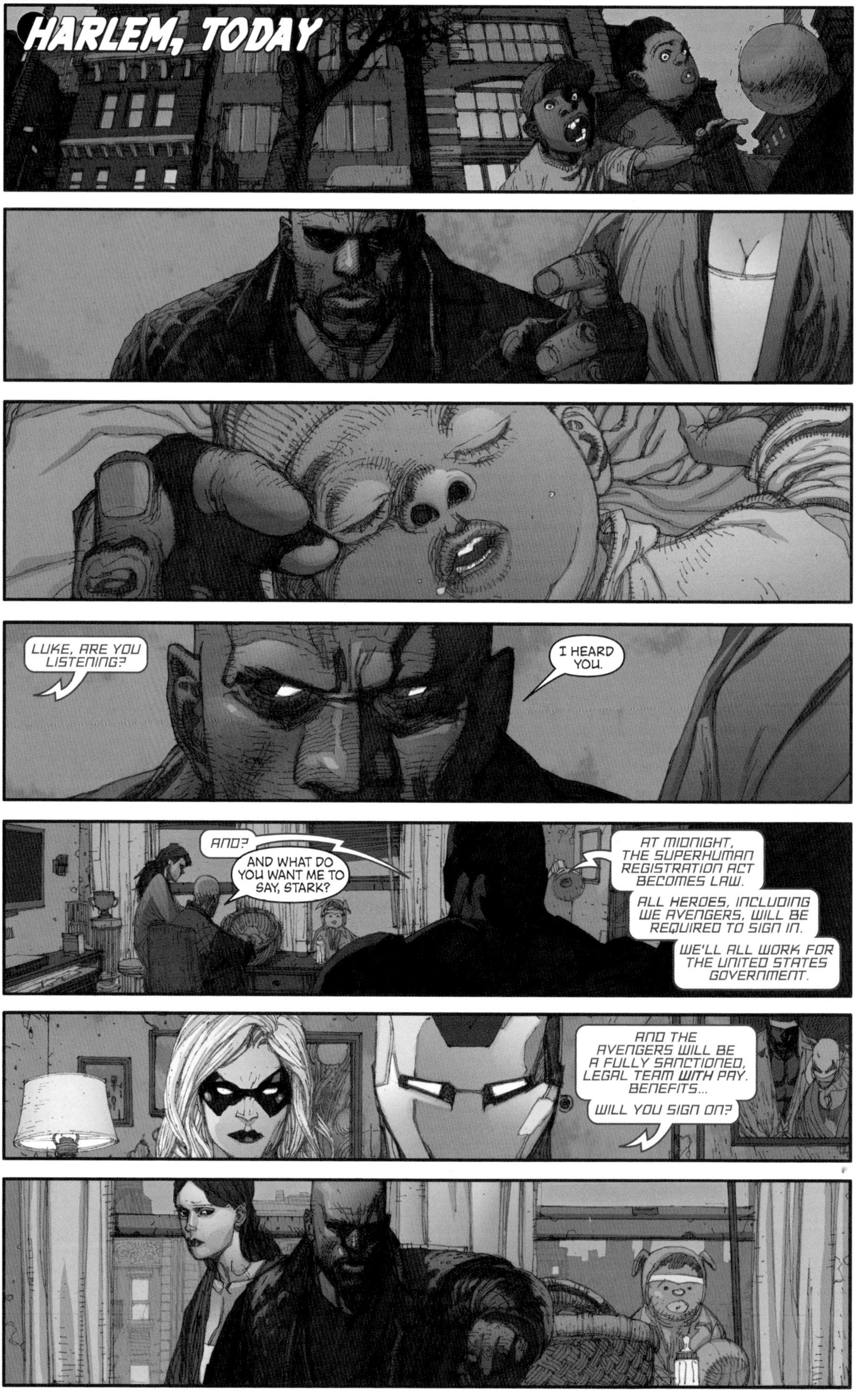
HARLEM, TODAY
LUKE, ARE YOU LISTENING?
I HEARD YOU.
AND?
AND WHAT DO YOU WANT ME TO SAY, STARK?
AT MIDNIGHT, THE SUPERHUMAN REGISTRATION ACT BECOMES LAW.
ALL HEROES, INCLUDING WE AVENGERS, WILL BE REQUIRED TO SIGN IN.
WE'LL ALL WORK FOR THE UNITED STATES GOVERNMENT.
AND THE AVENGERS WILL BE A FULLY SANCTIONED, LEGAL TEAM WITH PAY. BENEFITS...
WILL YOU SIGN ON?

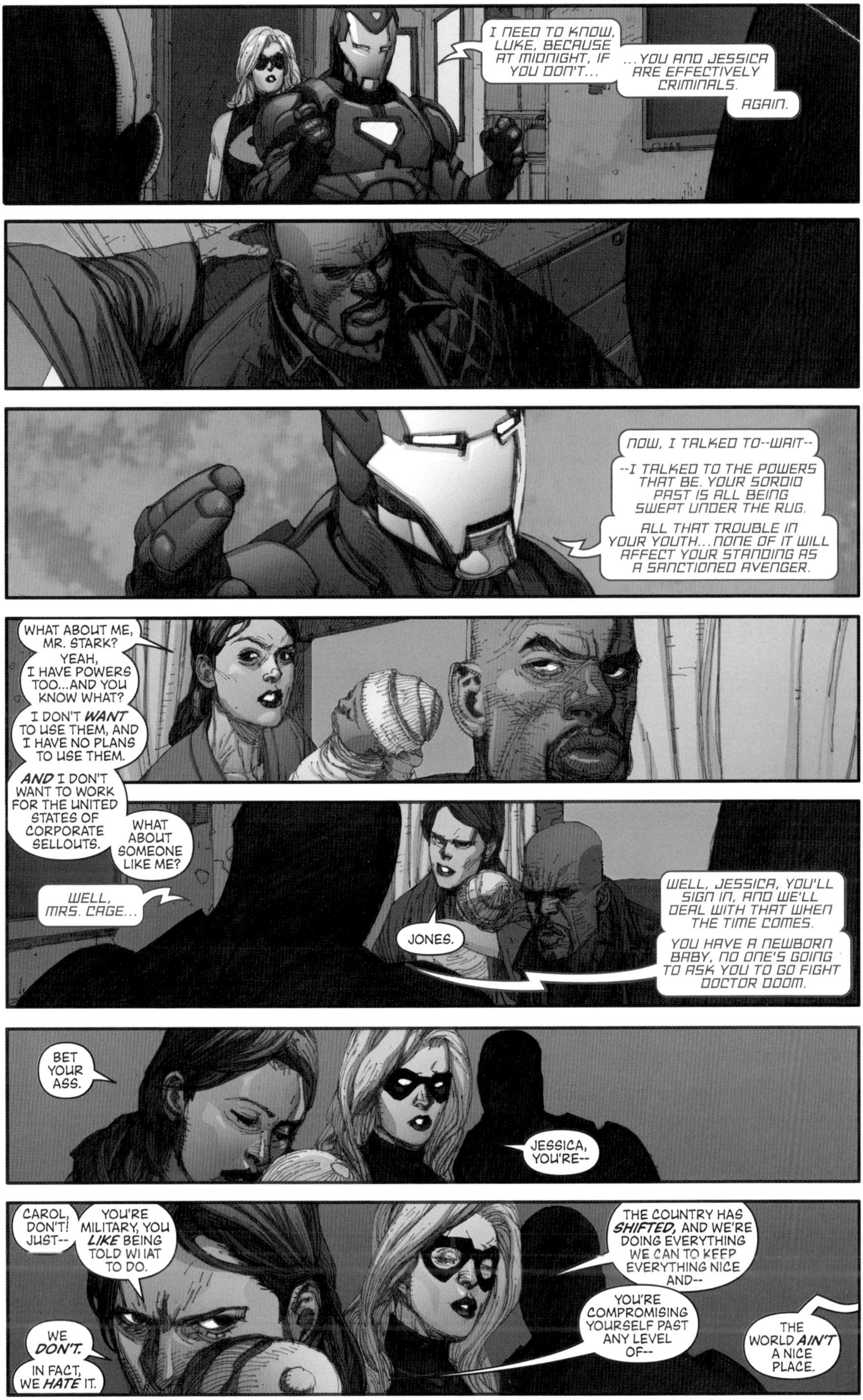
I NEED TO KNOW, LUKE, BECAUSE AT MIDNIGHT, IF YOU DON'T...
...YOU AND JESSICA ARE EFFECTIVELY CRIMINALS.
AGAIN.
NOW, I TALKED TO--WAIT--
--I TALKED TO THE POWERS THAT BE. YOUR SORDID PAST IS ALL BEING SWEPT UNDER THE RUG.
ALL THAT TROUBLE IN YOUR YOUTH... NONE OF IT WILL AFFECT YOUR STANDING AS A SANCTIONED AVENGER.
WHAT ABOUT ME, MR. STARK?
YEAH, I HAVE POWERS TOO...AND YOU KNOW WHAT?
I DON'T WANT TO USE THEM, AND I HAVE NO PLANS TO USE THEM.
AND I DON'T WANT TO WORK FOR THE UNITED STATES OF CORPORATE SELLOUTS.
WHAT ABOUT SOMEONE LIKE ME?
WELL, MRS. CAGE...
JONES.
WELL, JESSICA, YOU'LL SIGN IN, AND WE'LL DEAL WITH THAT WHEN THE TIME COMES.
YOU HAVE A NEWBORN BABY, NO ONE'S GOING TO ASK YOU TO GO FIGHT DOCTOR DOOM.
BET YOUR ASS.
JESSICA, YOU'RE--
YOU'RE MILITARY, YOU LIKE BEING TOLD WHAT TO DO.
CAROL, DON'T! JUST--
WE DON'T. IN FACT, WE HATE IT.
THE COUNTRY HAS SHIFTED, AND WE'RE DOING EVERYTHING WE CAN TO KEEP EVERYTHING NICE AND--
YOU'RE COMPROMISING YOURSELF PAST ANY LEVEL OF--
THE WORLD AIN'T A NICE PLACE.

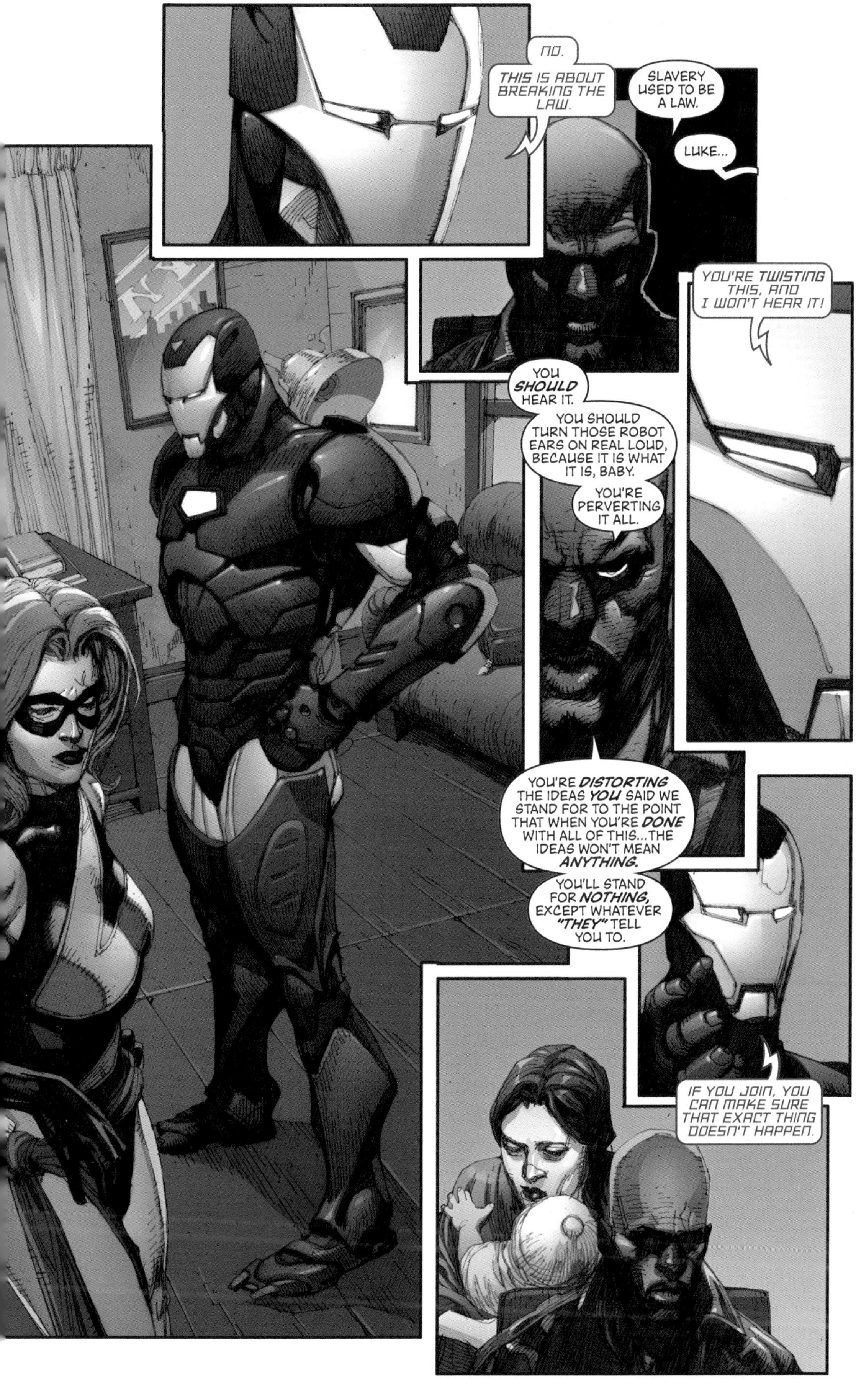
NO.
THIS IS ABOUT BREAKING THE LAW.
SLAVERY USED TO BE A LAW.
LUKE...
YOU'RE TWISTING THIS, AND I WON'T HEAR IT!
YOU SHOULD HEAR IT.
YOU SHOULD TURN THOSE ROBOT EARS ON REAL LOUD, BECAUSE IT IS WHAT IT IS, BABY.
YOU'RE PERVERTING IT ALL.
YOU'RE DISTORTING THE IDEAS YOU SAID WE STAND FOR TO THE POINT THAT WHEN YOU'RE DONE WITH ALL OF THIS...THE IDEAS WON'T MEAN ANYTHING.
YOU'LL STAND FOR NOTHING, EXCEPT WHATEVER "THEY" TELL YOU TO.
IF YOU JOIN, YOU CAN MAKE SURE THAT EXACT THING DOESN'T HAPPEN.

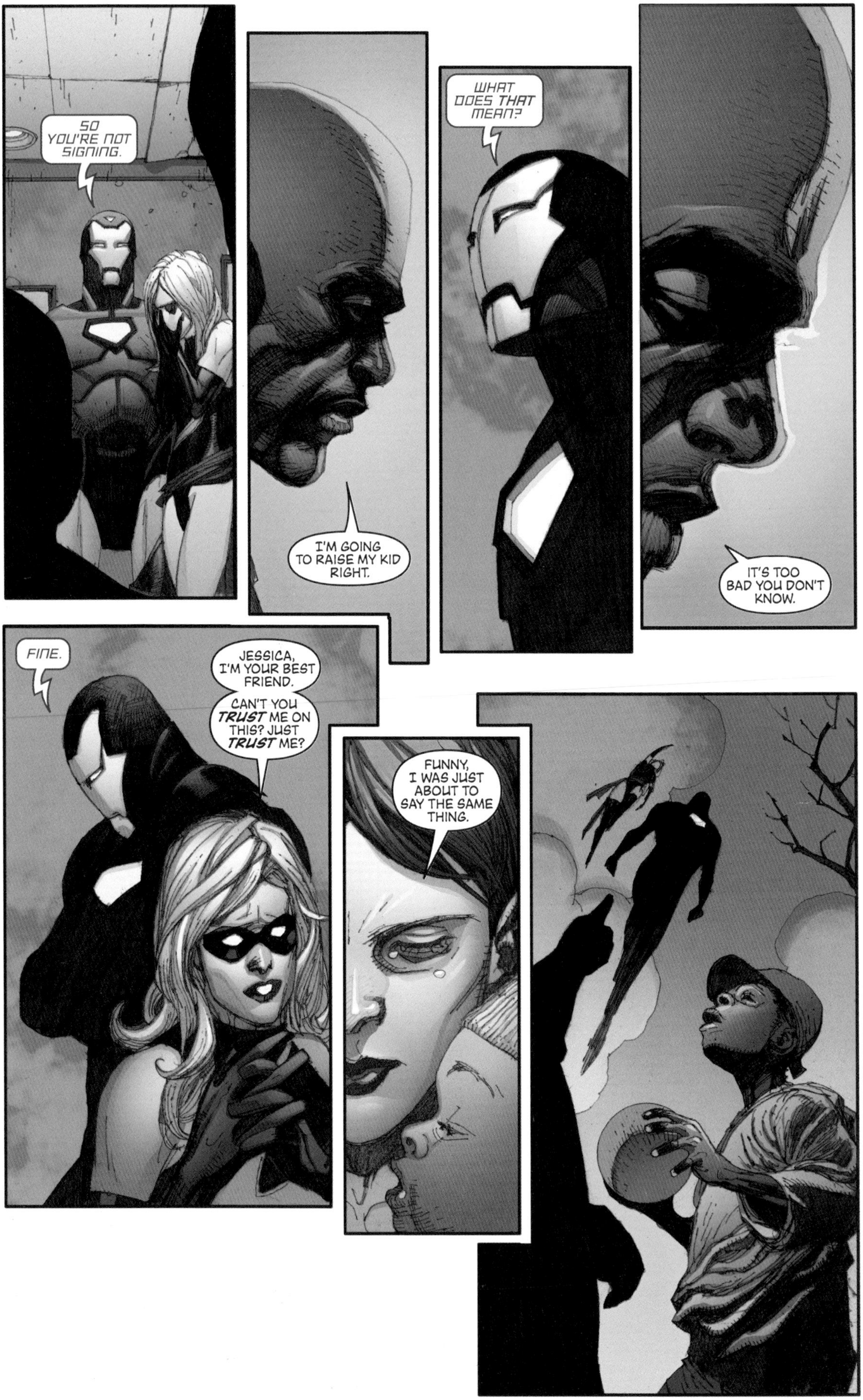
SO YOU'RE NOT SIGNING.
I'M GOING TO RAISE MY KID RIGHT.
WHAT DOES THAT MEAN?
IT'S TOO BAD YOU DON'T KNOW.
FINE.
JESSICA, I'M YOUR BEST FRIEND.
CAN'T YOU TRUST ME ON THIS? JUST TRUST ME?
FUNNY, I WAS JUST ABOUT TO SAY THE SAME THING.

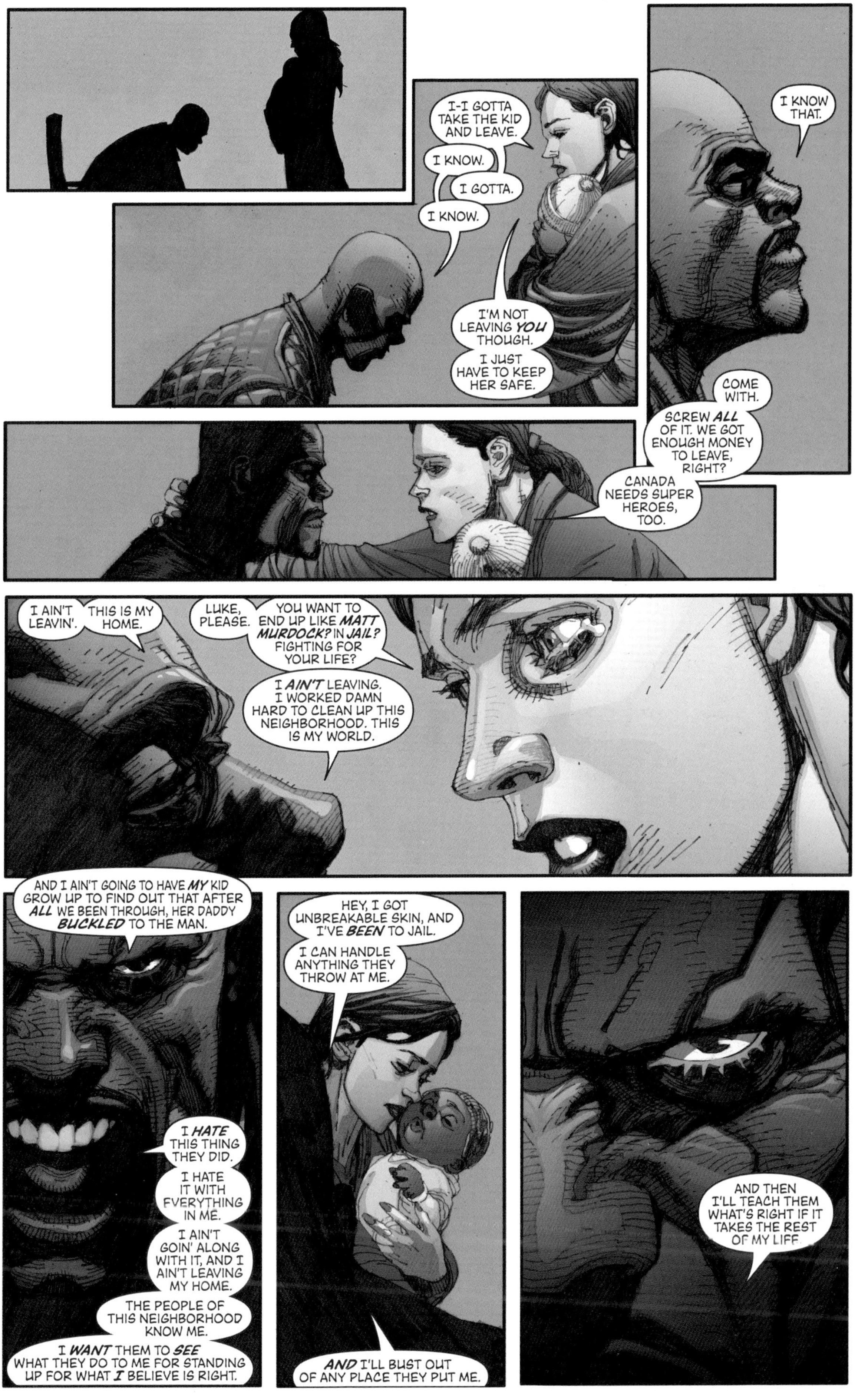
I-I GOTTA TAKE THE KID AND LEAVE.
I KNOW.
I GOTTA.
I KNOW.
I'M NOT LEAVING YOU THOUGH.
I JUST HAVE TO KEEP HER SAFE.
I KNOW THAT.
COME WITH.
SCREW ALL OF IT. WE GOT ENOUGH MONEY TO LEAVE, RIGHT?
CANADA NEEDS SUPER HEROES, TOO.
I AIN'T LEAVIN'.
THIS IS MY HOME.
LUKE, PLEASE.
YOU WANT TO END UP LIKE MATT MURDOCK? IN JAIL? FIGHTING FOR YOUR LIFE?
I AIN'T LEAVING. I WORKED DAMN HARD TO CLEAN UP THIS NEIGHBORHOOD. THIS IS MY WORLD.
AND I AIN'T GOING TO HAVE MY KID GROW UP TO FIND OUT THAT AFTER ALL WE BEEN THROUGH, HER DADDY BUCKLED TO THE MAN.
I HATE THIS THING THEY DID.
I HATE IT WITH EVERYTHING IN ME.
I AIN'T GOIN' ALONG WITH IT, AND I AIN'T LEAVING MY HOME.
THE PEOPLE OF THIS NEIGHBORHOOD KNOW ME.
I WANT THEM TO SEE WHAT THEY DO TO ME FOR STANDING UP FOR WHAT I BELIEVE IS RIGHT.
HEY, I GOT UNBREAKABLE SKIN, AND I'VE BEEN TO JAIL.
I CAN HANDLE ANYTHING THEY THROW AT ME.
AND I'LL BUST OUT OF ANY PLACE THEY PUT ME.
AND THEN I'LL TEACH THEM WHAT'S RIGHT IF IT TAKES THE REST OF MY LIFE.

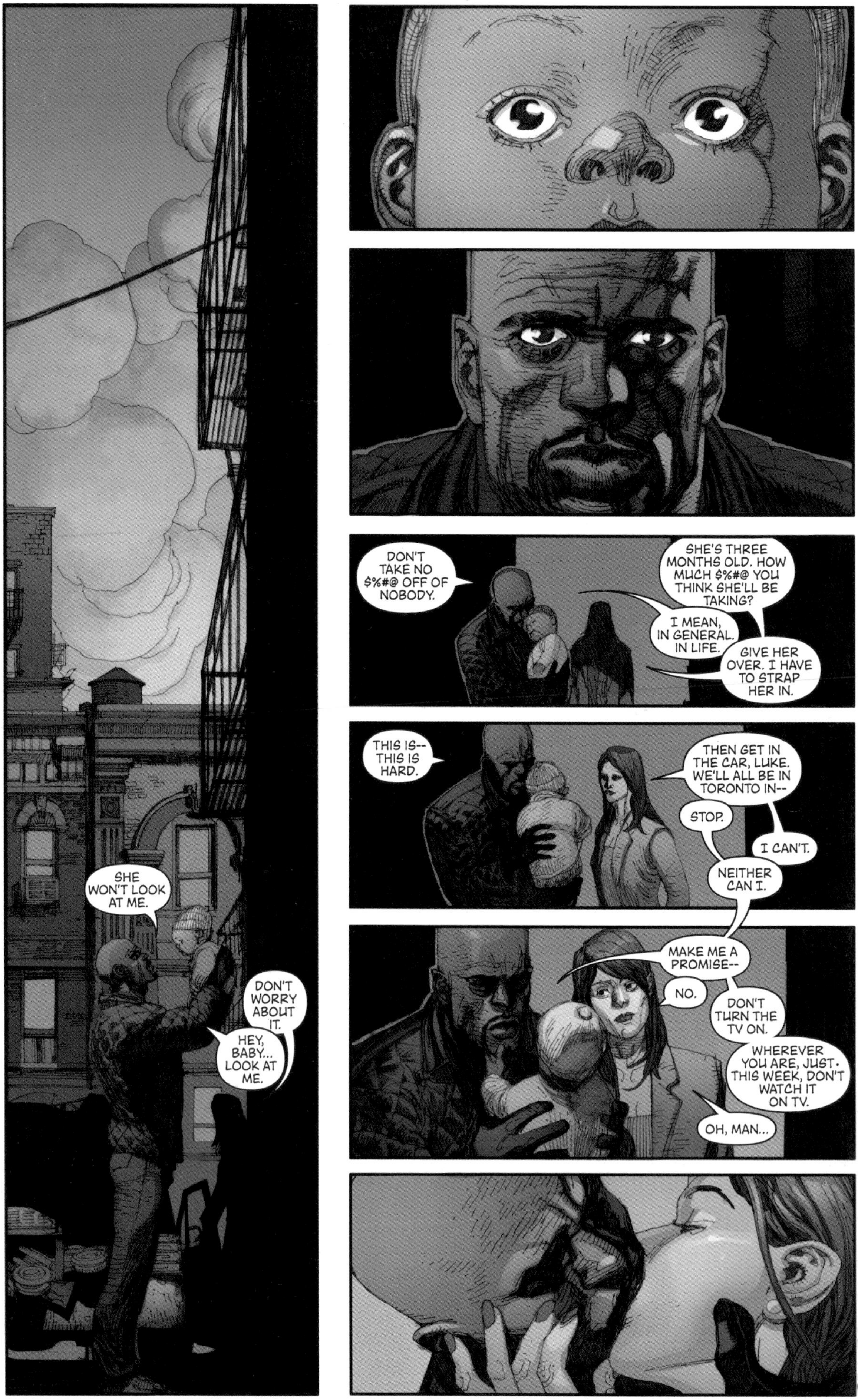
SHE WON'T LOOK AT ME.
DON'T WORRY ABOUT IT.
HEY, BABY... LOOK AT ME.
DON'T TAKE NO $%#@ OFF OF NOBODY.
SHE'S THREE MONTHS OLD. HOW MUCH $%#@ YOU THINK SHE'LL BE TAKING?
I MEAN, IN GENERAL. IN LIFE.
GIVE HER OVER. I HAVE TO STRAP HER IN.
THIS IS-- THIS IS HARD.
THEN GET IN THE CAR, LUKE. WE'LL ALL BE IN TORONTO IN--
STOP.
I CAN'T.
NEITHER CAN I.
MAKE ME A PROMISE--
NO.
DON'T TURN THE TV ON.
WHEREVER YOU ARE, JUST. THIS WEEK, DON'T WATCH IT ON TV.
OH, MAN...

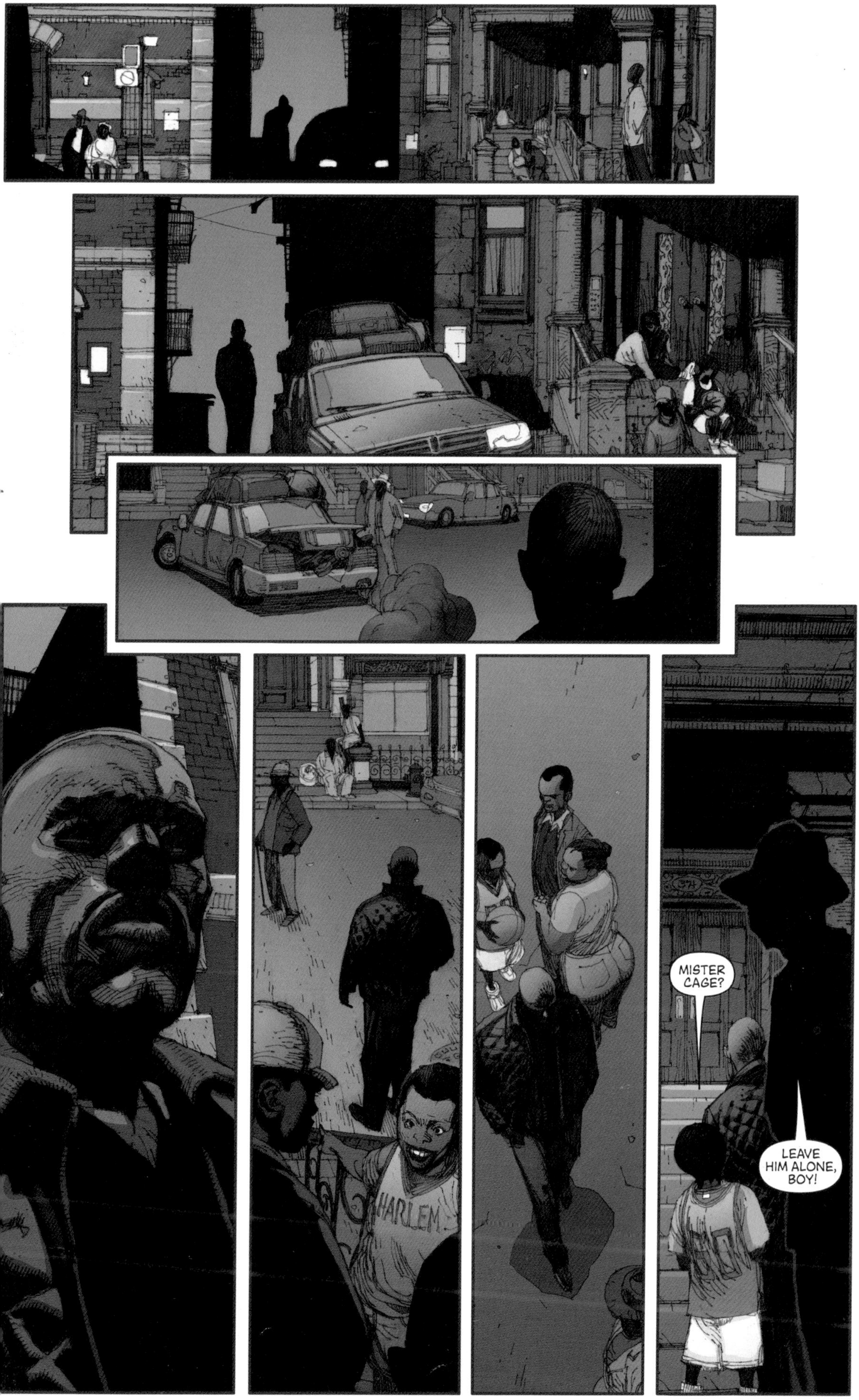
MISTER CAGE?
LEAVE HIM ALONE, BOY!

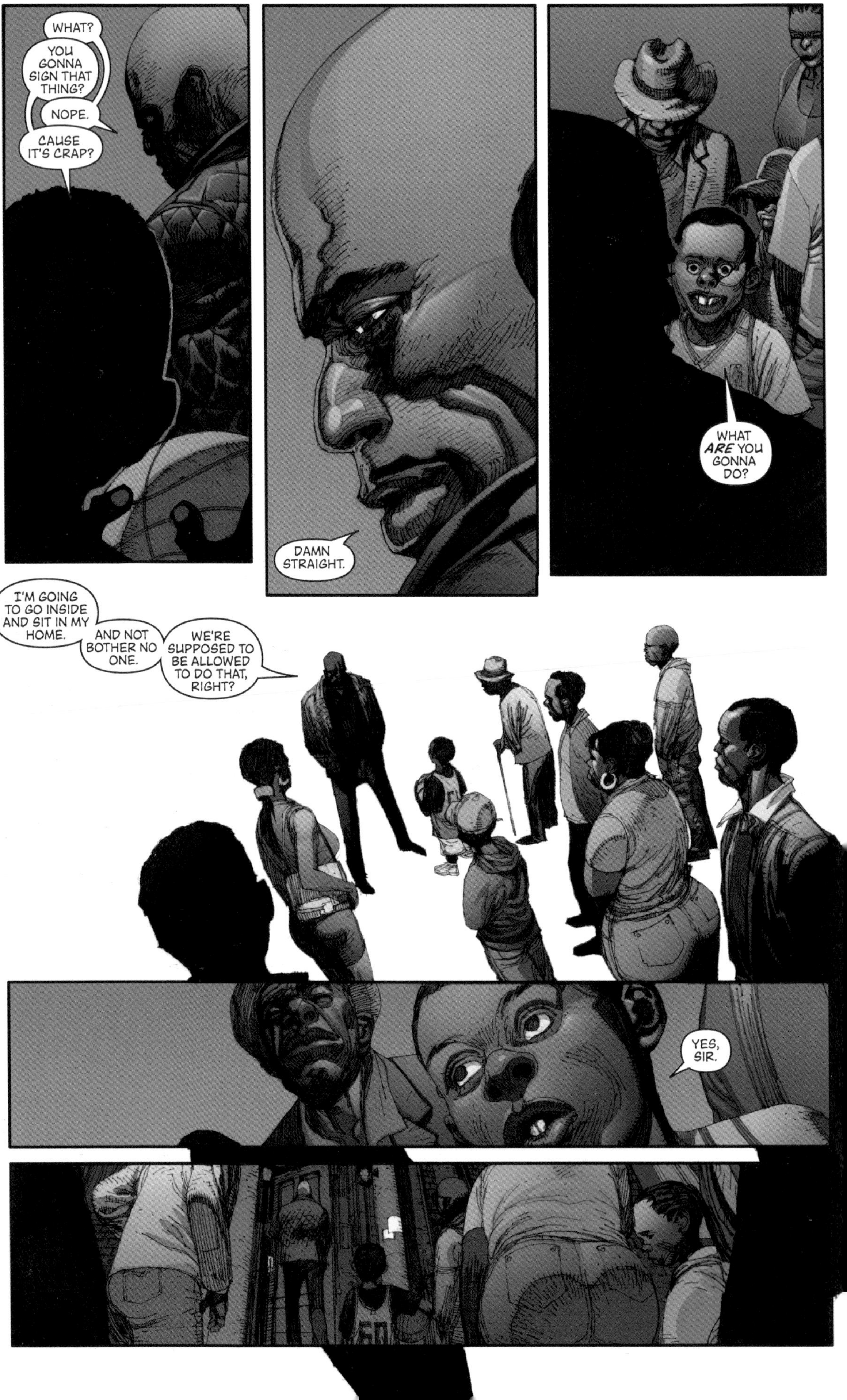
WHAT?
YOU GONNA SIGN THAT THING?
NOPE.
CAUSE IT'S CRAP?
DAMN STRAIGHT.
WHAT **ARE** YOU GONNA DO?
I'M GOING TO GO INSIDE AND SIT IN MY HOME.
AND NOT BOTHER NO ONE.
WE'RE SUPPOSED TO BE ALLOWED TO DO THAT, RIGHT?
YES, SIR.

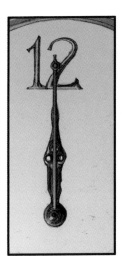

MISTER CAGE?

INCREDIBLE.

MISTER CAGE, THIS IS S.H.I.E.L.D. AGENT GABRIEL JONES. CAN I HAVE A WORD WITH YOU, PLEASE?

I'M KIND OF IN THE MIDDLE OF SOMETHING.

CAN YOU COME BACK ANOTHER TIME?

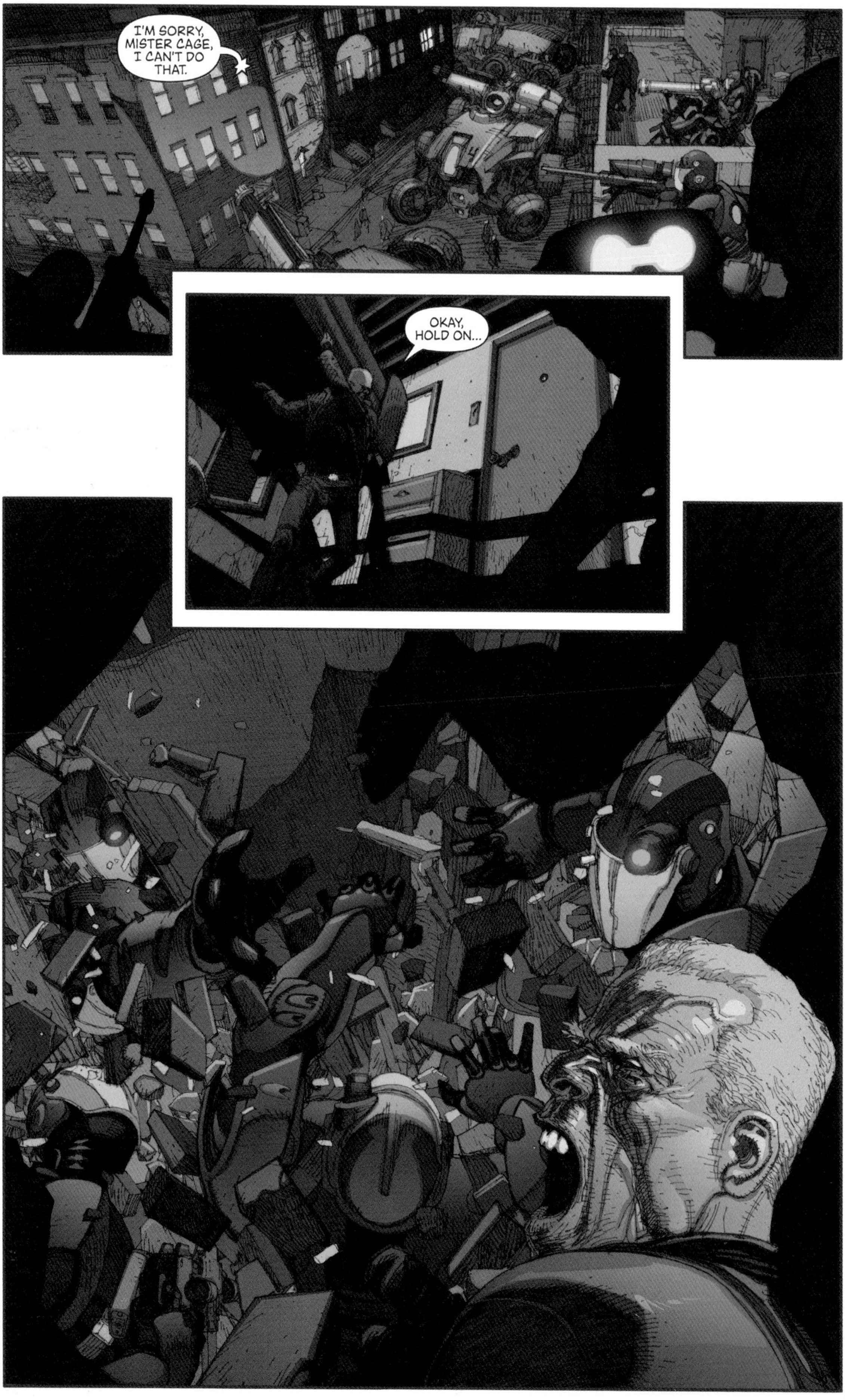
I'M SORRY, MISTER CAGE, I CAN'T DO THAT.
OKAY, HOLD ON...

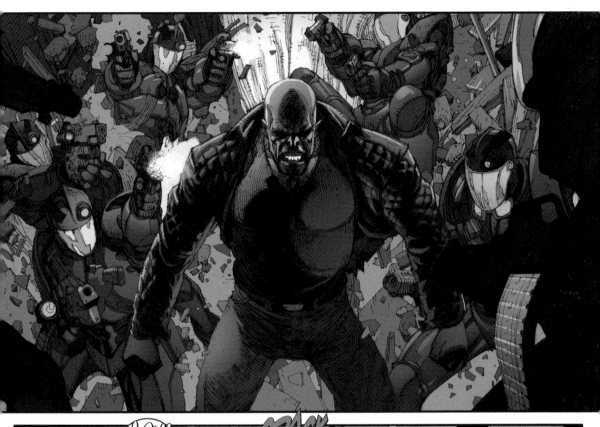

AGH!

CRACK

AGH!

DIRECT HIT!

FSSRAAMMM

FSSRAAMMM

THIS IS TEAM COBRA. CAGE IS DOWN.

LUCAS CAGE, MY NAME IS S.H.I.E.L.D. AGENT WHITMAN. YOU ARE UNDER ARREST FOR VIOLATING THE FEDERAL SUPERHUMAN REGISTRATION ACT.

IT IS MY DUTY TO INFORM YOU THAT YOU HAVE THE RIGHT TO REMAIN SILENT. IF YOU GIVE UP THAT RIGHT, ANYTHING YOU SAY--

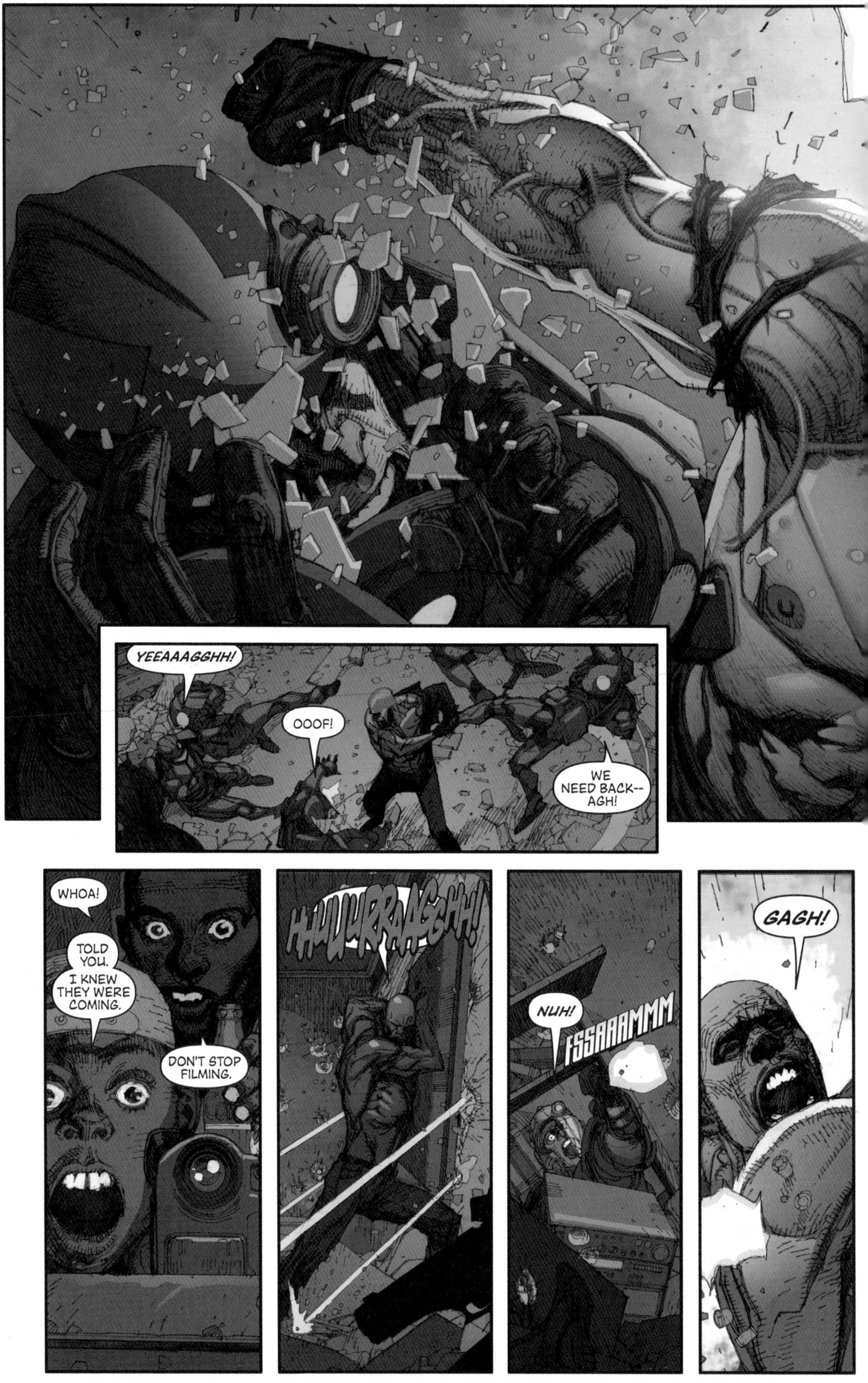
YEEAAAGGHH!
OOOF!
WE NEED BACK-- AGH!
WHOA!
TOLD YOU. I KNEW THEY WERE COMING.
DON'T STOP FILMING.
HHUUURRAAGGHH!
NUH!
FSSAAAMMM
GAGH!

YEAH, YEAH! I REMEMBER IT FROM THE LAST TIME I WAS FALSELY ACCUSED OF #$%^ I DIDN'T DO!!

AGH!

OKAY, WE GOT A PROBLEM IN HERE!

SMASH

HELICARRIER. WE ARE EXPERIENCING RESISTANCE.

GROUND CREW ROMAN! GET IN THERE.

THE HALLWAY IS BLOCKED.

USE YOUR HOVER DISCS.

KEEP AN EYE ON THE SKY. IT MIGHT BE AN AMBUSH.

IT'S JUST ONE GUY?

FSSRAAMMM FSSRAAMMM FSSRAAMMM

ARGH!

FSSRAAMMM FSSRAAMMM FSSRAAMMM

FSSRAAMMM FSSRAAMMM

FSSRAAMMM FSSRAAMMM

DON'T LET HIM--!

FSSRAAMMM FSSRAAMMM

FSSRAAMMM FSSRAAMMM

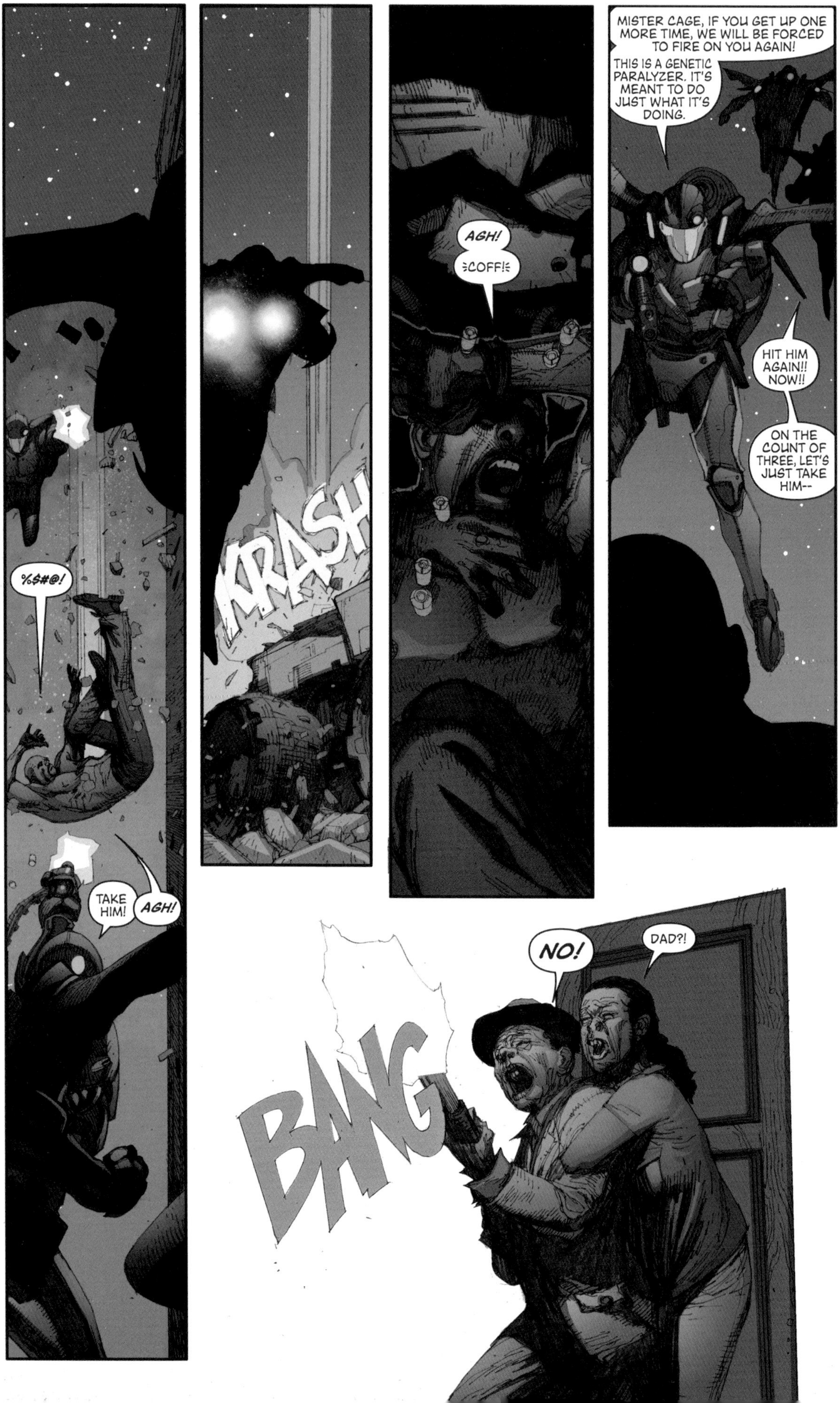
%$#@!
TAKE HIM!
AGH!
KRASH
AGH!
COFF!
MISTER CAGE, IF YOU GET UP ONE MORE TIME, WE WILL BE FORCED TO FIRE ON YOU AGAIN!
THIS IS A GENETIC PARALYZER. IT'S MEANT TO DO JUST WHAT IT'S DOING.
HIT HIM AGAIN!! NOW!!
ON THE COUNT OF THREE, LET'S JUST TAKE HIM--
BANG
NO!
DAD?!

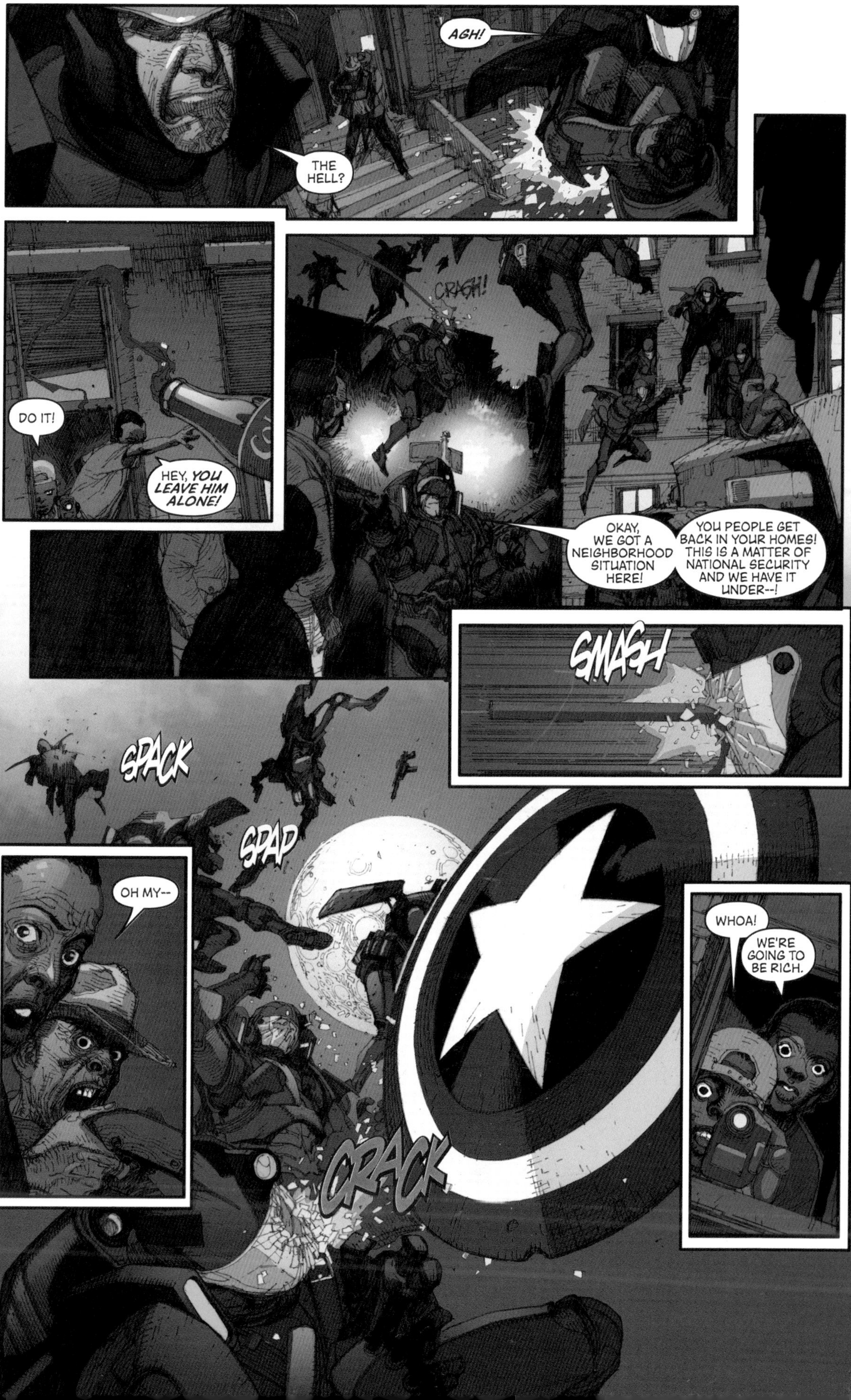
AGH!
THE HELL?
DO IT!
HEY, YOU LEAVE HIM ALONE!
CRASH!
OKAY, WE GOT A NEIGHBORHOOD SITUATION HERE!
YOU PEOPLE GET BACK IN YOUR HOMES! THIS IS A MATTER OF NATIONAL SECURITY AND WE HAVE IT UNDER--!
SMASH
SPACK
SPAP
OH MY--
WHOA!
WE'RE GOING TO BE RICH.
CRACK

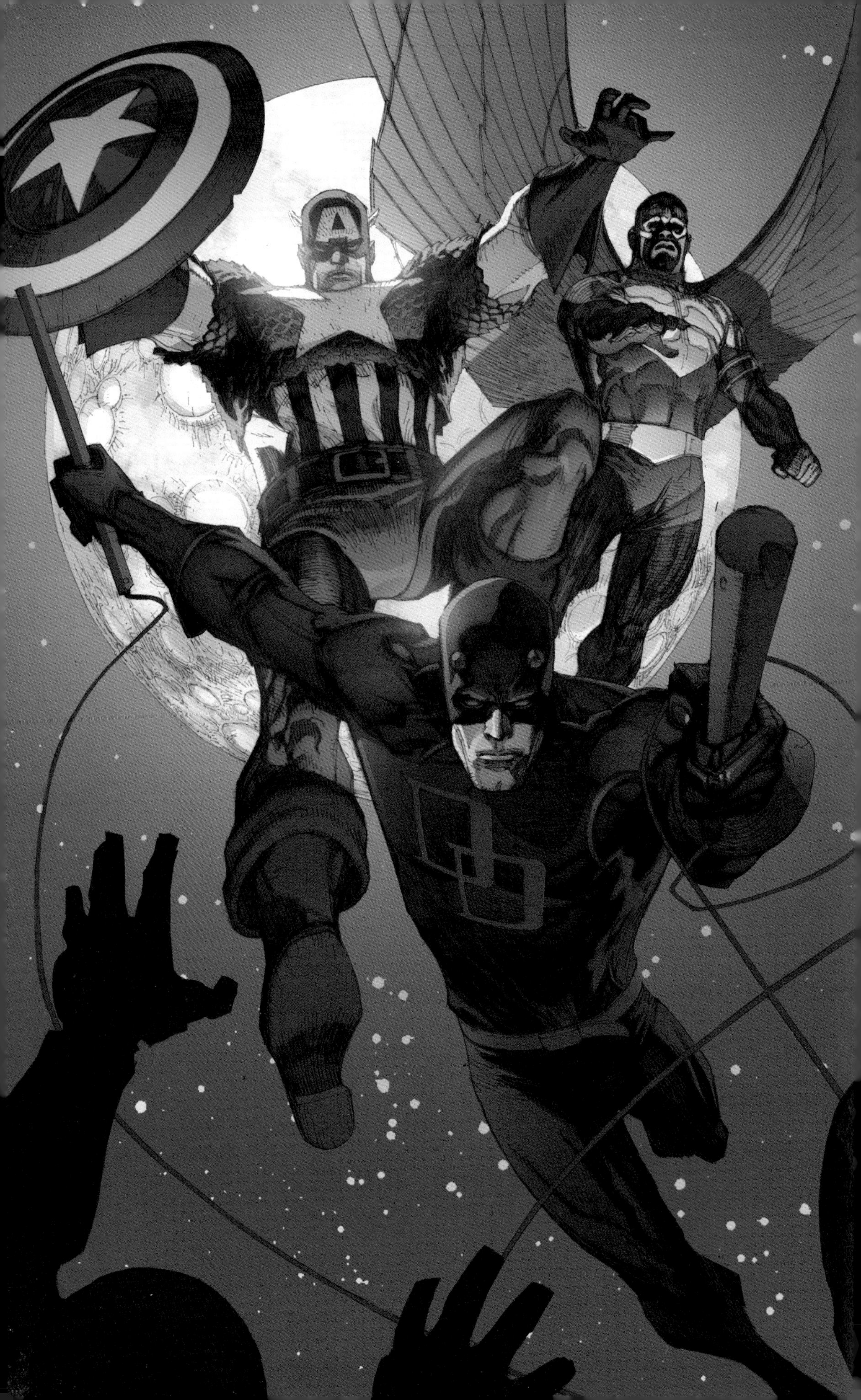

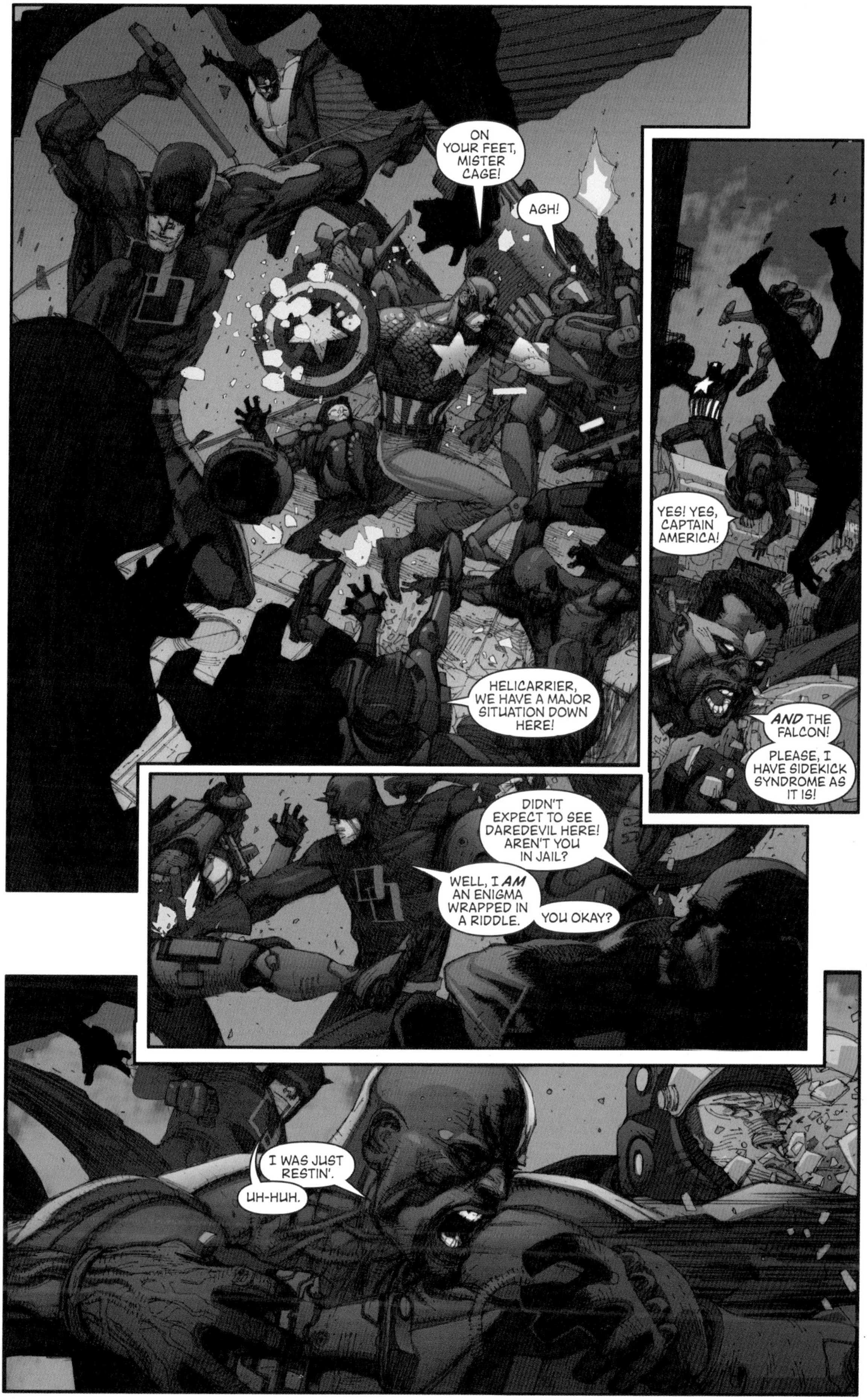
ON YOUR FEET, MISTER CAGE!
AGH!
HELICARRIER, WE HAVE A MAJOR SITUATION DOWN HERE!
YES! YES, CAPTAIN AMERICA!
AND THE FALCON!
PLEASE, I HAVE SIDEKICK SYNDROME AS IT IS!
DIDN'T EXPECT TO SEE DAREDEVIL HERE! AREN'T YOU IN JAIL?
WELL, I AM AN ENIGMA WRAPPED IN A RIDDLE.
YOU OKAY?
I WAS JUST RESTIN'.
UH-HUH.

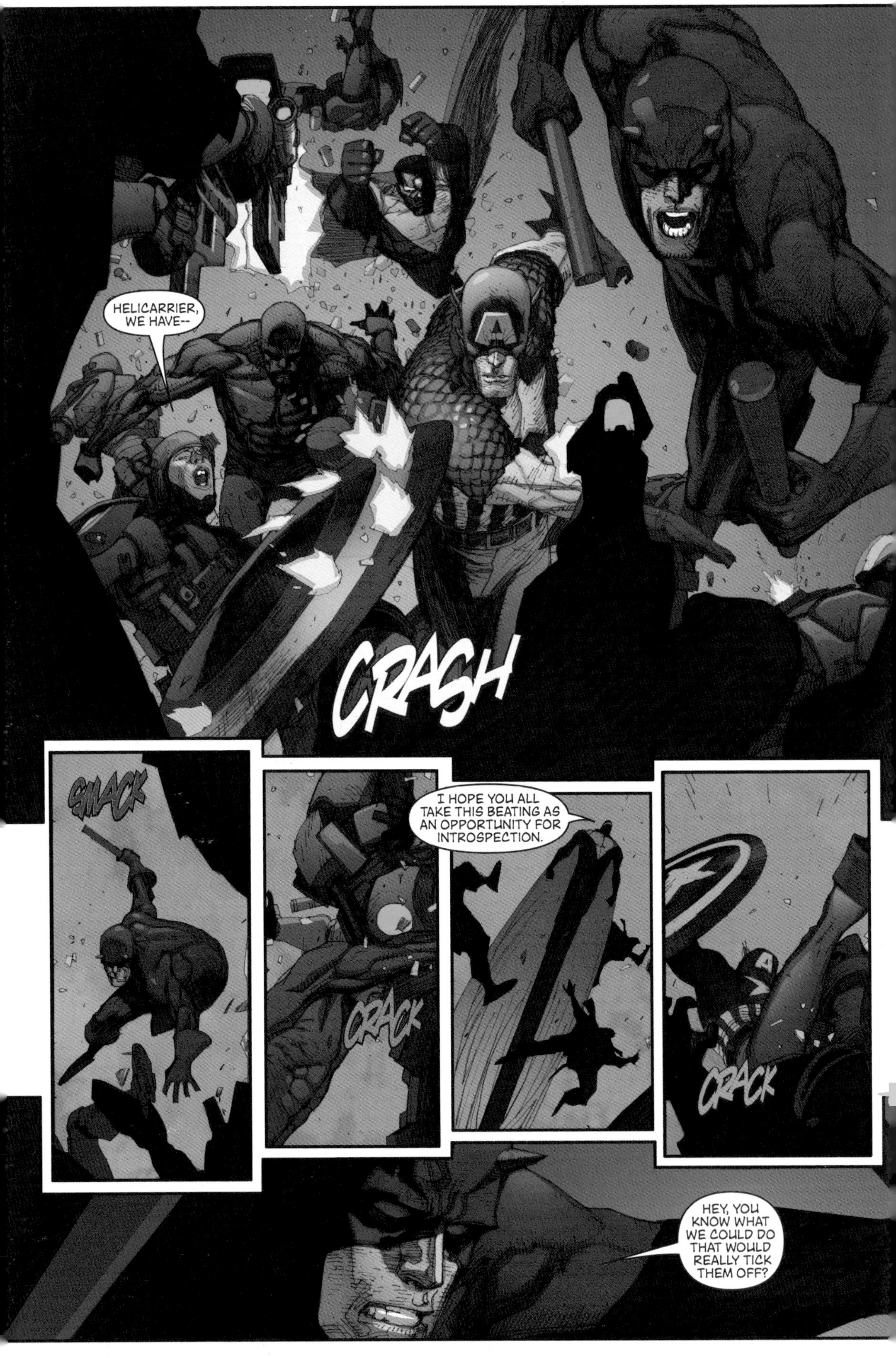
HELICARRIER, WE HAVE--
CRASH
SMACK
CRACK
I HOPE YOU ALL TAKE THIS BEATING AS AN OPPORTUNITY FOR INTROSPECTION.
CRACK
HEY, YOU KNOW WHAT WE COULD DO THAT WOULD REALLY TICK THEM OFF?

SCREEEEEEEEEEEEEEEEEEEEEEL

HELICARRIER ONE, THEY ARE FLEEING. WE DON'T HAVE CLEARANCE FOR A STREET PURSUIT, OVER?

THEY WHO?

YO! HELICARRIER, THIS IS LUKE CAGE, HOW Y'ALL DOIN' TONIGHT?

FANCY.

CAGE, THIS IS MARIA HILL, YOU'RE JUST MAKING IT WORSE FOR YOURSELF!

WE CAN TRACK THAT VEHICLE ANYWHERE YOU GO WITH IT.

YEAH, KINDA FIGURED, BUT...

WE JUST WANTED Y'ALL TO KNOW.

THE REVOLUTION IS COMING.

BZZT

REVOLUTION?

YEAH, I DIDN'T KNOW WHAT ELSE TO SAY.

JESSICA AND THE BABY?

SENT THEM TO TORONTO.

GOOD.

GOOD DIM SUM THERE.

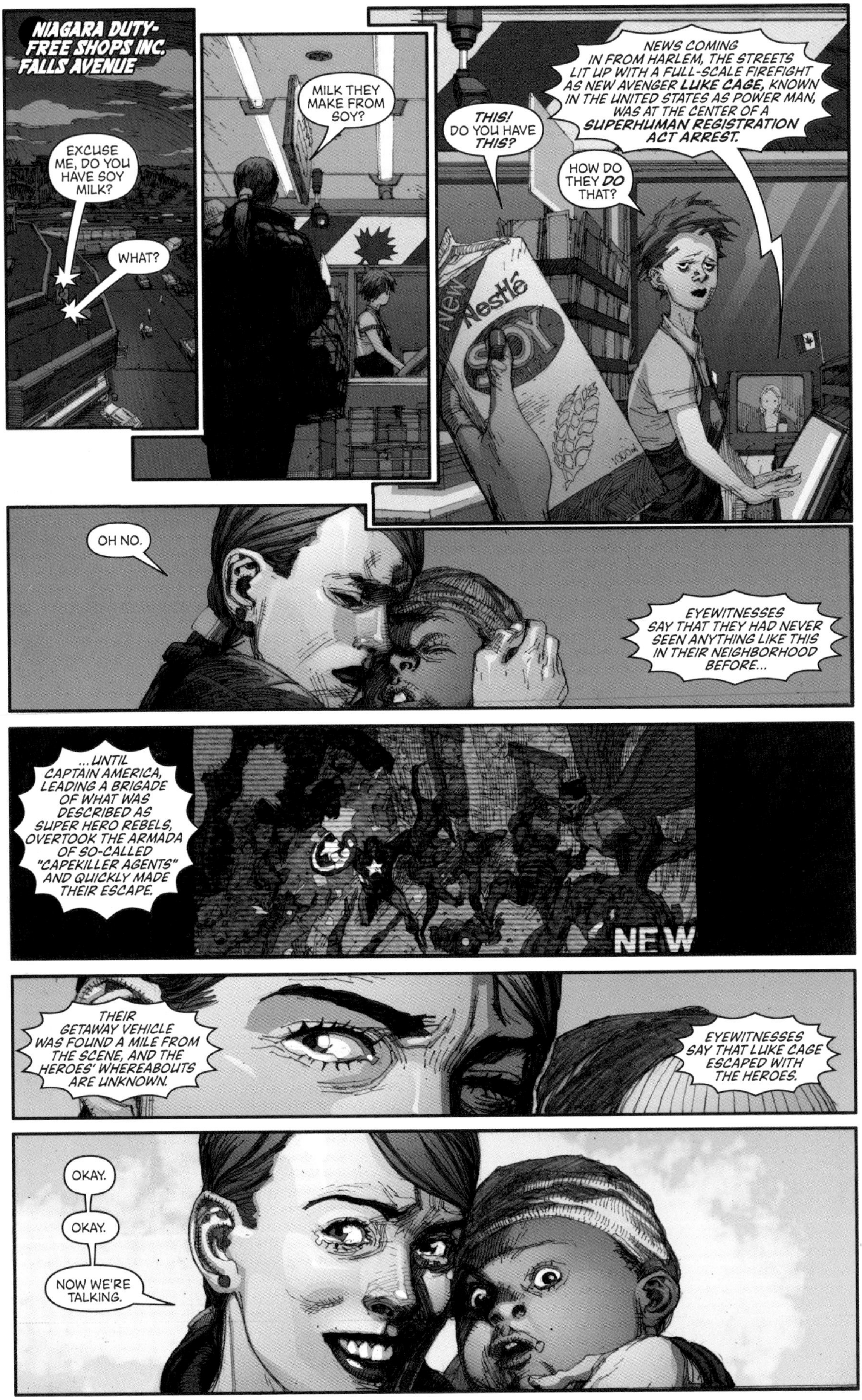
NIAGARA DUTY-FREE SHOPS INC. FALLS AVENUE
EXCUSE ME, DO YOU HAVE SOY MILK?
WHAT?
MILK THEY MAKE FROM SOY?
THIS! DO YOU HAVE THIS?
NEWS COMING IN FROM HARLEM, THE STREETS LIT UP WITH A FULL-SCALE FIREFIGHT AS NEW AVENGER LUKE CAGE, KNOWN IN THE UNITED STATES AS POWER MAN, WAS AT THE CENTER OF A SUPERHUMAN REGISTRATION ACT ARREST.
HOW DO THEY DO THAT?
New Nestlé SOY
OH NO.
EYEWITNESSES SAY THAT THEY HAD NEVER SEEN ANYTHING LIKE THIS IN THEIR NEIGHBORHOOD BEFORE...
...UNTIL CAPTAIN AMERICA, LEADING A BRIGADE OF WHAT WAS DESCRIBED AS SUPER HERO REBELS, OVERTOOK THE ARMADA OF SO-CALLED "CAPEKILLER AGENTS" AND QUICKLY MADE THEIR ESCAPE.
NEW
THEIR GETAWAY VEHICLE WAS FOUND A MILE FROM THE SCENE, AND THE HEROES' WHEREABOUTS ARE UNKNOWN.
EYEWITNESSES SAY THAT LUKE CAGE ESCAPED WITH THE HEROES.
OKAY.
OKAY.
NOW WE'RE TALKING.

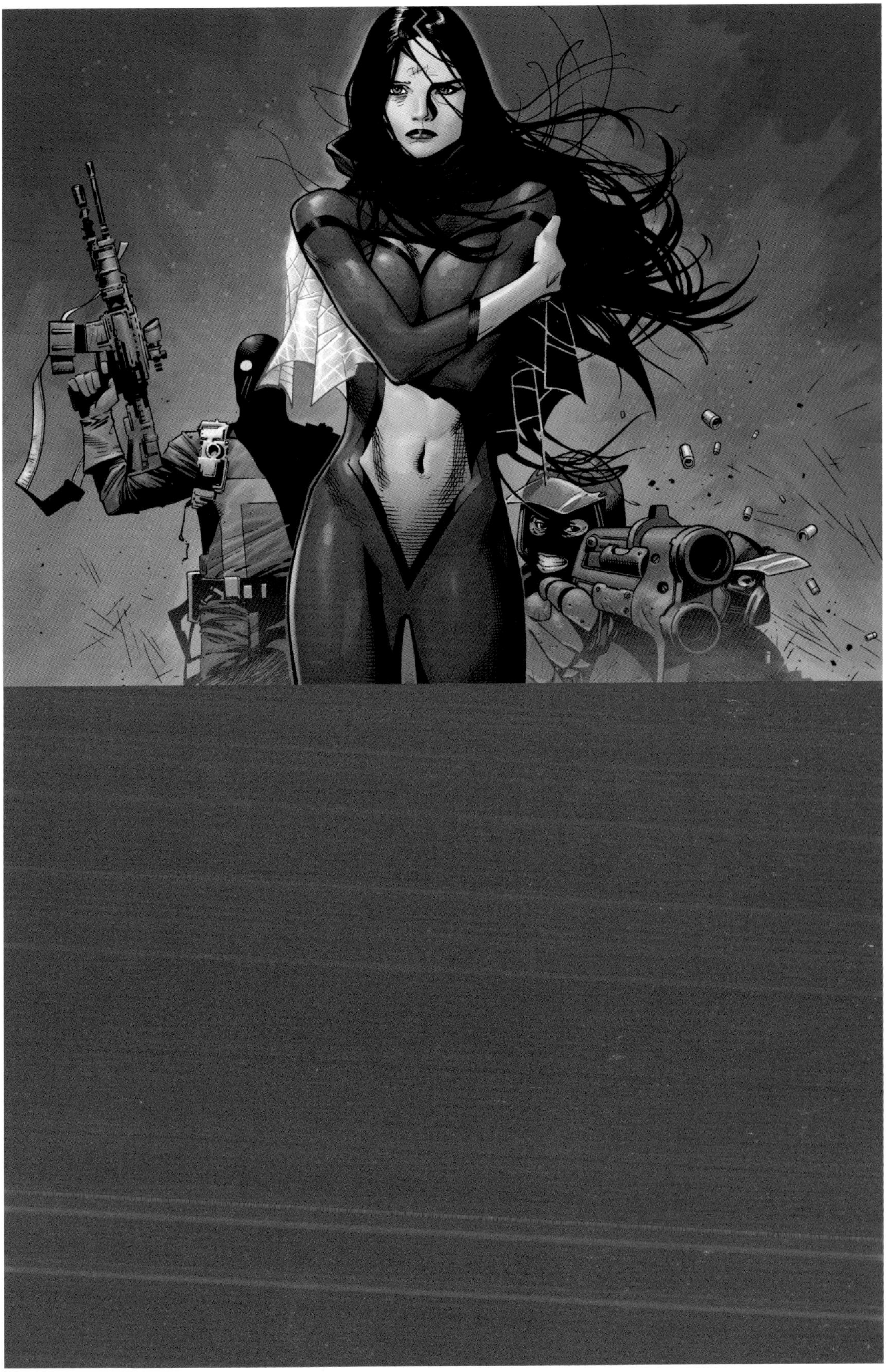

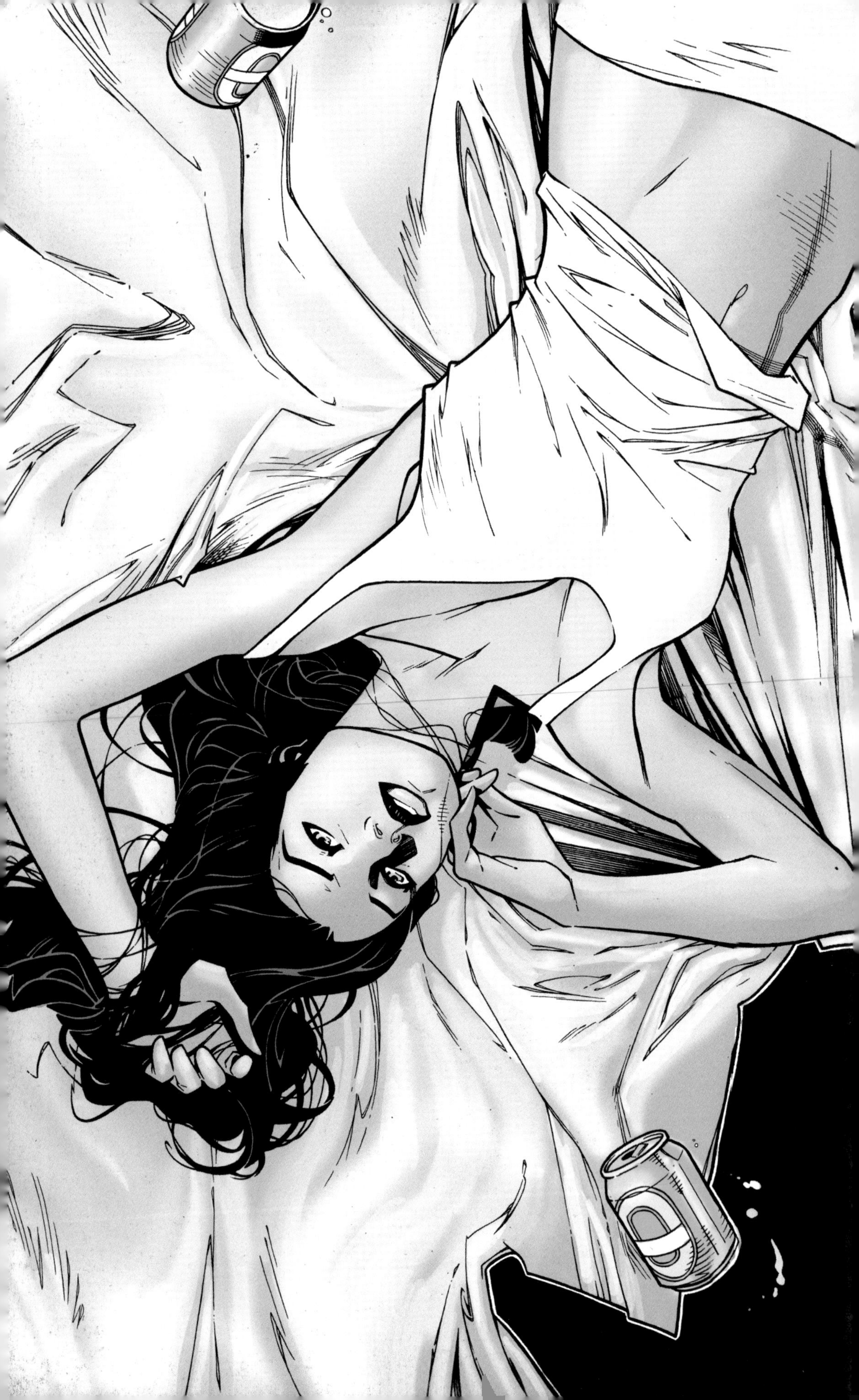

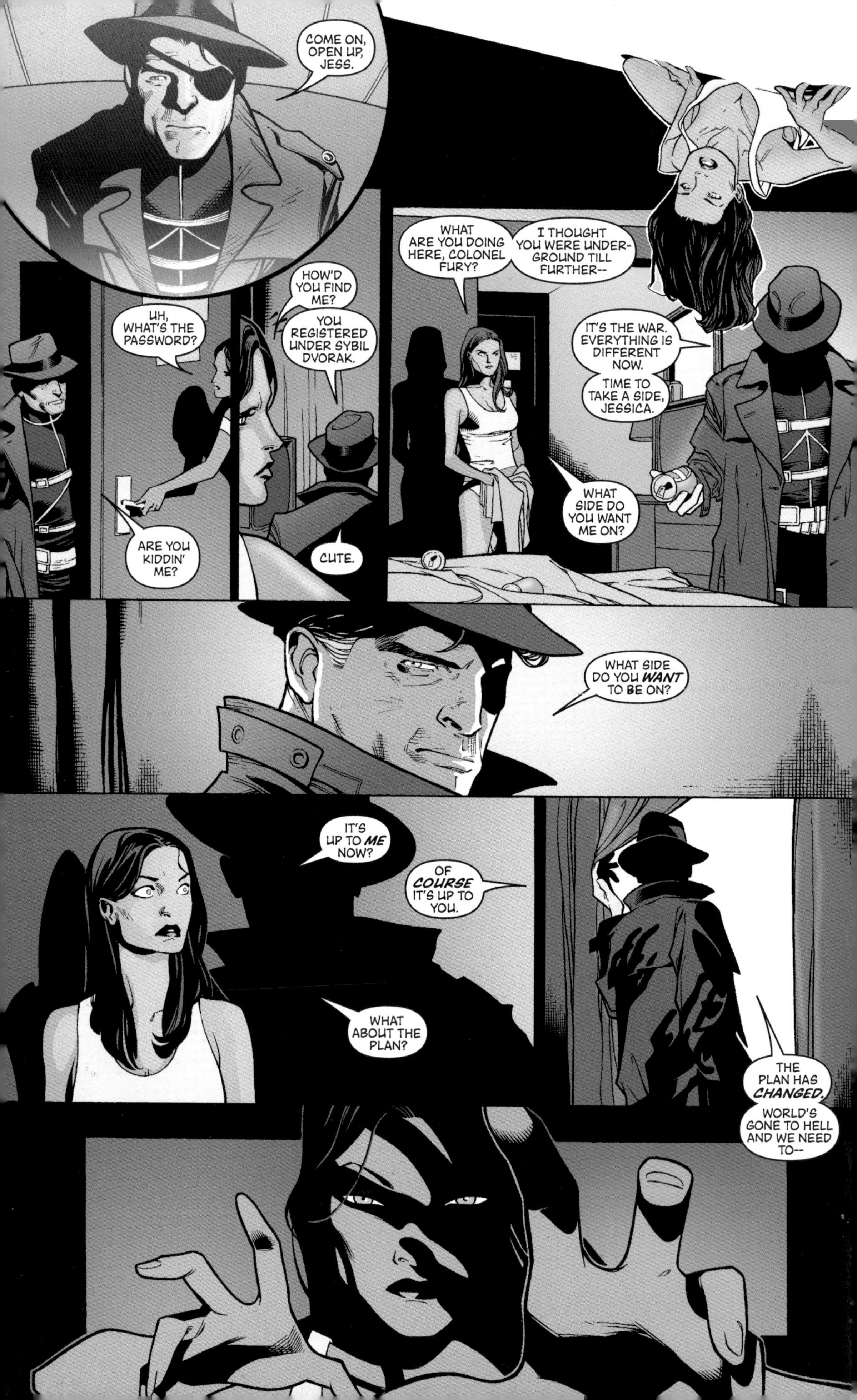
COME ON, OPEN UP, JESS.
UH, WHAT'S THE PASSWORD?
ARE YOU KIDDIN' ME?
HOW'D YOU FIND ME?
YOU REGISTERED UNDER SYBIL DVORAK.
CUTE.
WHAT ARE YOU DOING HERE, COLONEL FURY?
I THOUGHT YOU WERE UNDER-GROUND TILL FURTHER--
IT'S THE WAR. EVERYTHING IS DIFFERENT NOW.
TIME TO TAKE A SIDE, JESSICA.
WHAT SIDE DO YOU WANT ME ON?
WHAT SIDE DO YOU *WANT* TO BE ON?
IT'S UP TO *ME* NOW?
OF *COURSE* IT'S UP TO YOU.
WHAT ABOUT THE PLAN?
THE PLAN HAS *CHANGED.*
WORLD'S GONE TO HELL AND WE NEED TO--

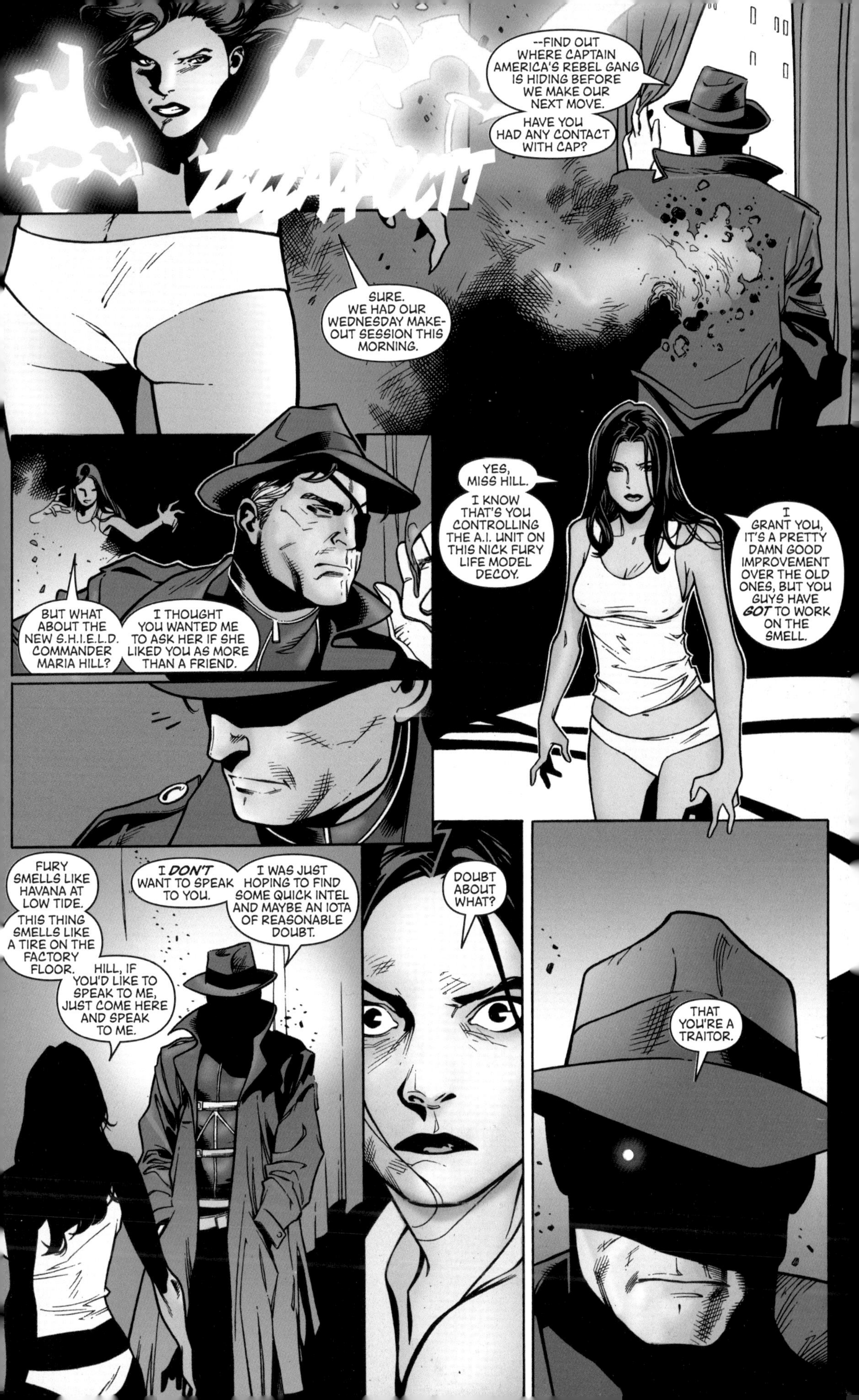

--FIND OUT WHERE CAPTAIN AMERICA'S REBEL GANG IS HIDING BEFORE WE MAKE OUR NEXT MOVE.
HAVE YOU HAD ANY CONTACT WITH CAP?
SURE. WE HAD OUR WEDNESDAY MAKE-OUT SESSION THIS MORNING.
BUT WHAT ABOUT THE NEW S.H.I.E.L.D. COMMANDER MARIA HILL?
I THOUGHT YOU WANTED ME TO ASK HER IF SHE LIKED YOU AS MORE THAN A FRIEND.
YES, MISS HILL.
I KNOW THAT'S YOU CONTROLLING THE A.I. UNIT ON THIS NICK FURY LIFE MODEL DECOY.
I GRANT YOU, IT'S A PRETTY DAMN GOOD IMPROVEMENT OVER THE OLD ONES, BUT YOU GUYS HAVE *GOT* TO WORK ON THE SMELL.
FURY SMELLS LIKE HAVANA AT LOW TIDE.
THIS THING SMELLS LIKE A TIRE ON THE FACTORY FLOOR.
HILL, IF YOU'D LIKE TO SPEAK TO ME, JUST COME HERE AND SPEAK TO ME.
I *DON'T* WANT TO SPEAK TO YOU.
I WAS JUST HOPING TO FIND SOME QUICK INTEL AND MAYBE AN IOTA OF REASONABLE DOUBT.
DOUBT ABOUT WHAT?
THAT YOU'RE A TRAITOR.

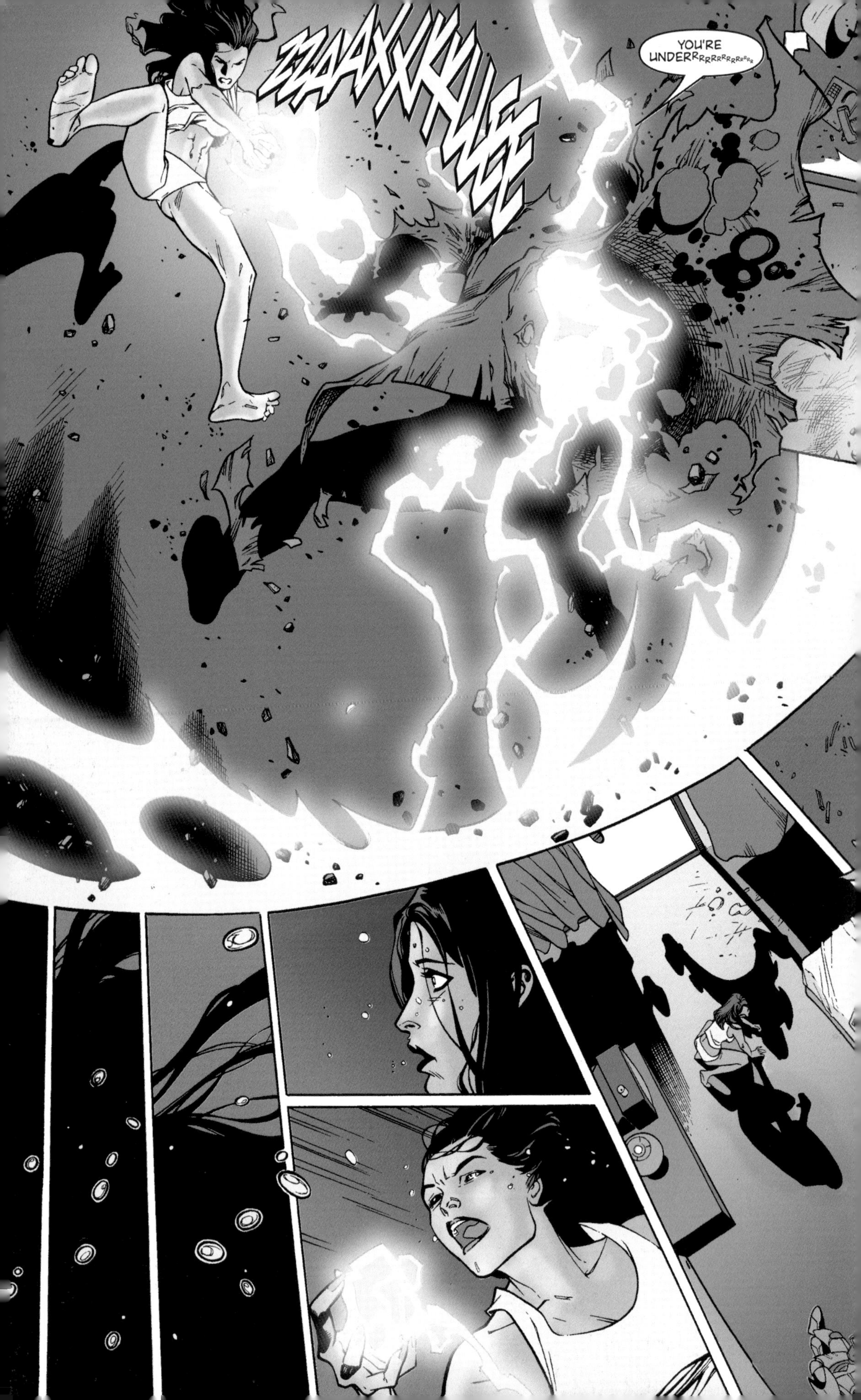
ZZAAAXXKKLLECE
YOU'RE UNDERRRRRRRRRRRR

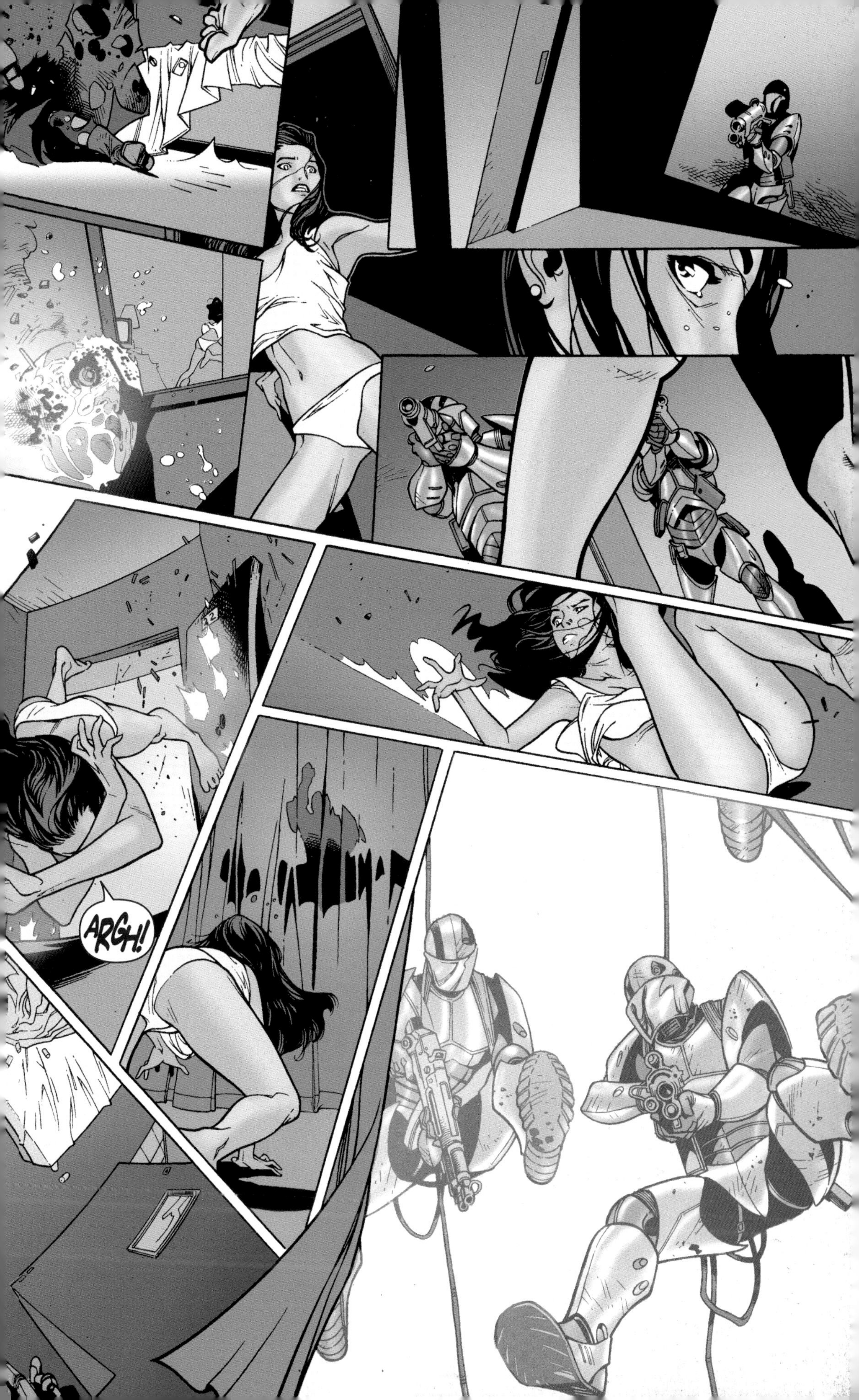
ARGH!

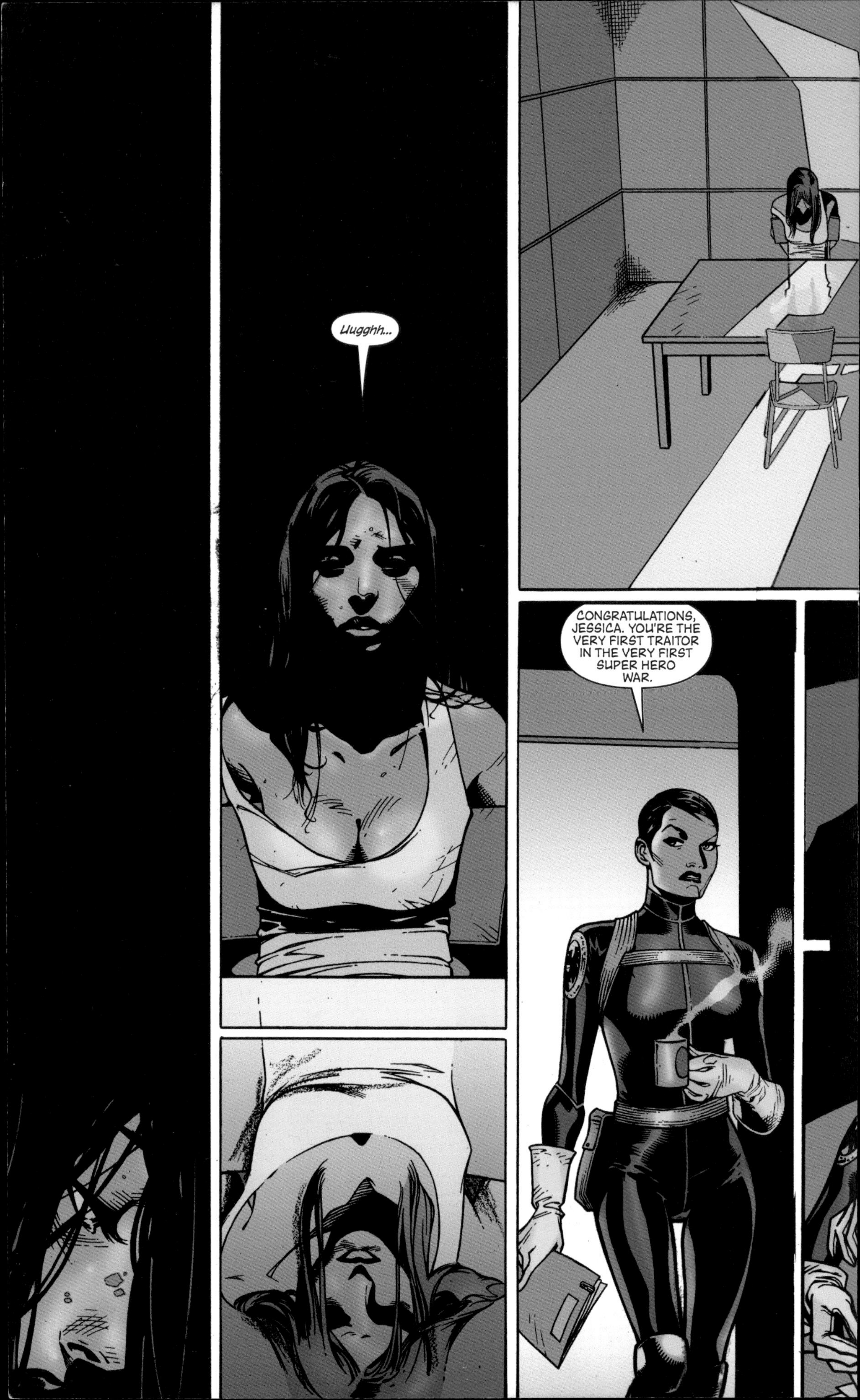
Uugghh...
CONGRATULATIONS, JESSICA. YOU'RE THE VERY FIRST TRAITOR IN THE VERY FIRST SUPER HERO WAR.

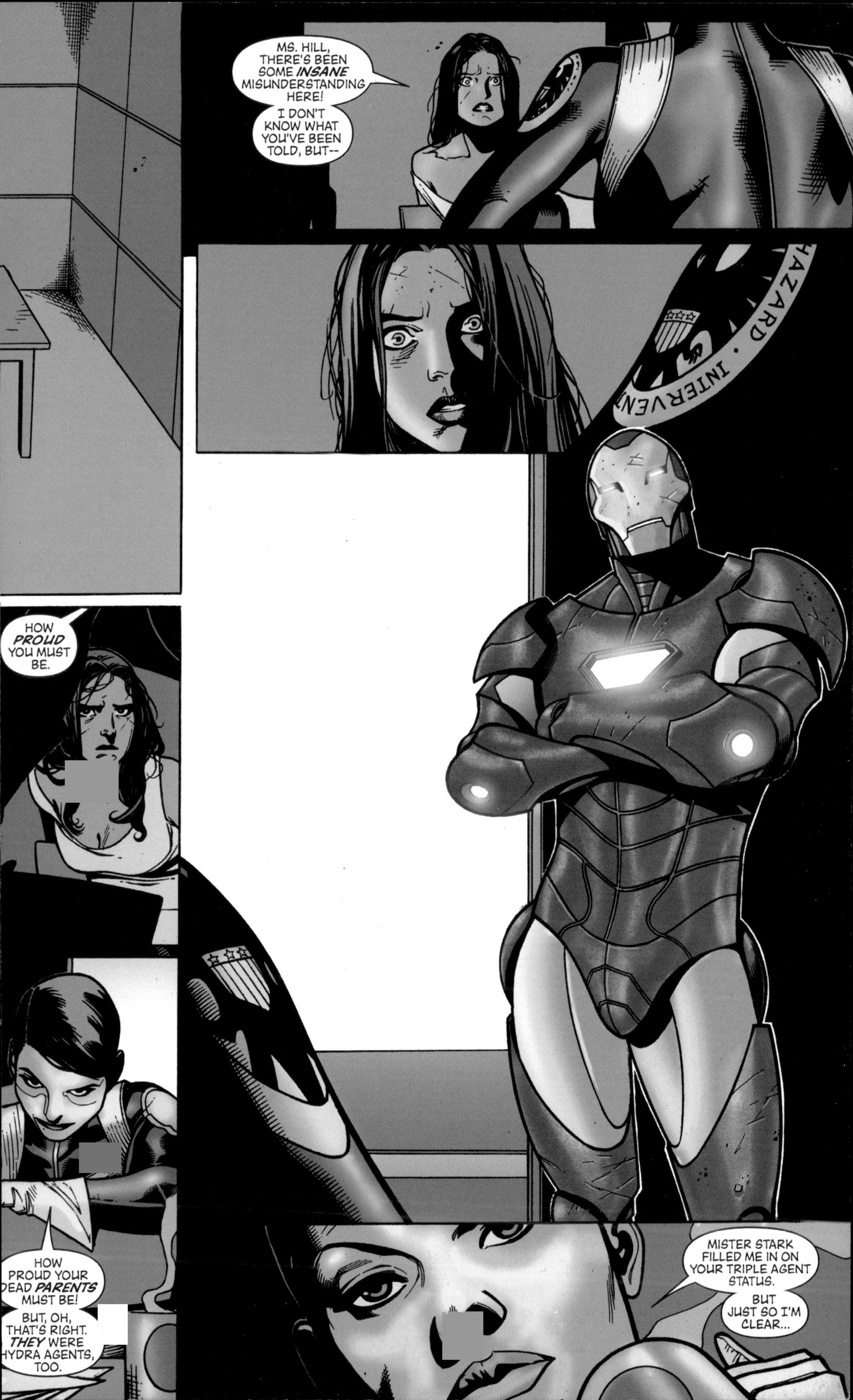
MS. HILL, THERE'S BEEN SOME *INSANE* MISUNDERSTANDING HERE!
I DON'T KNOW WHAT YOU'VE BEEN TOLD, BUT--
HAZARD
INTERVEN
HOW *PROUD* YOU MUST BE.
HOW PROUD YOUR DEAD *PARENTS* MUST BE!
BUT, OH, THAT'S RIGHT. *THEY* WERE HYDRA AGENTS, TOO.
MISTER STARK FILLED ME IN ON YOUR TRIPLE AGENT STATUS.
BUT JUST SO I'M CLEAR...

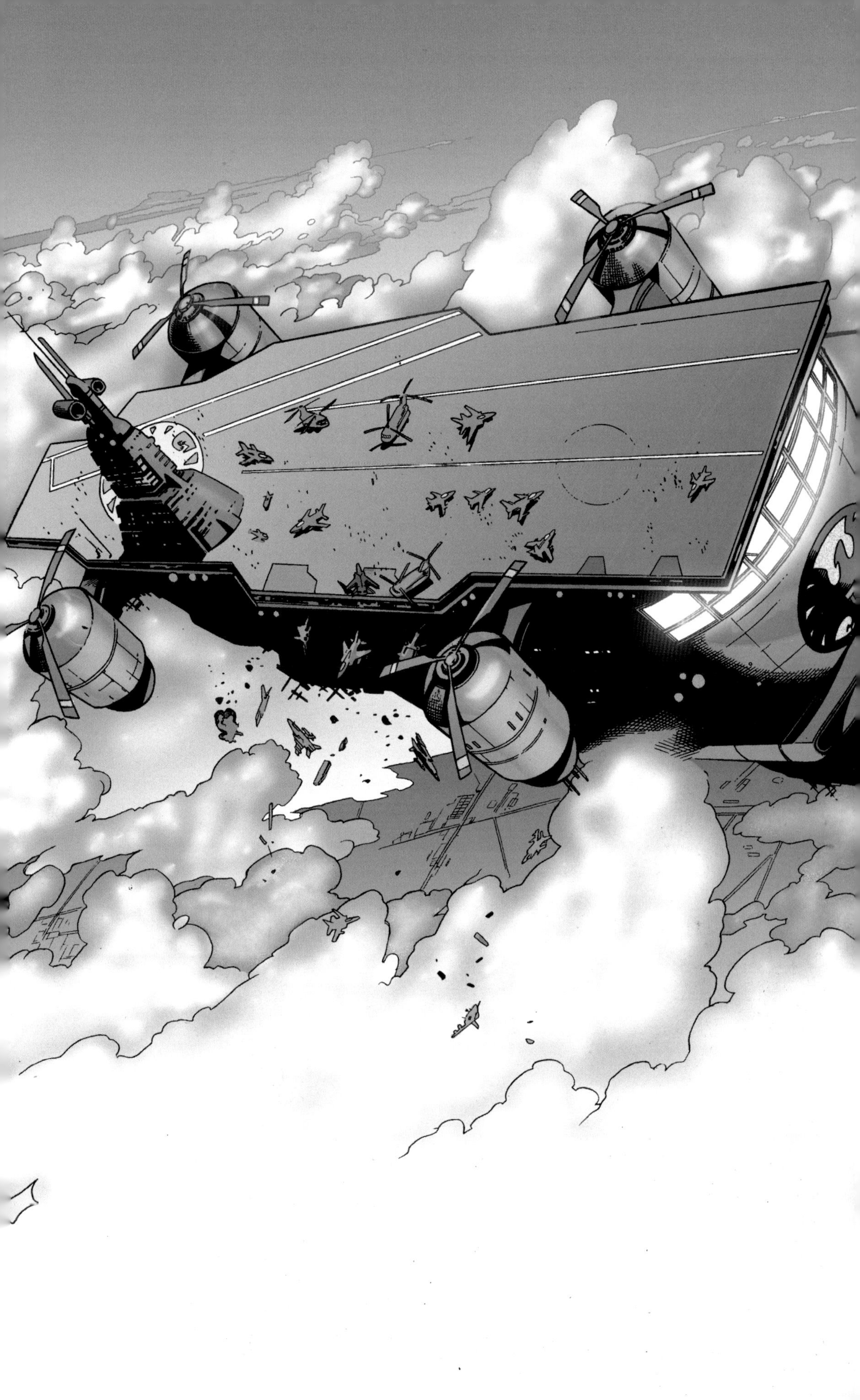

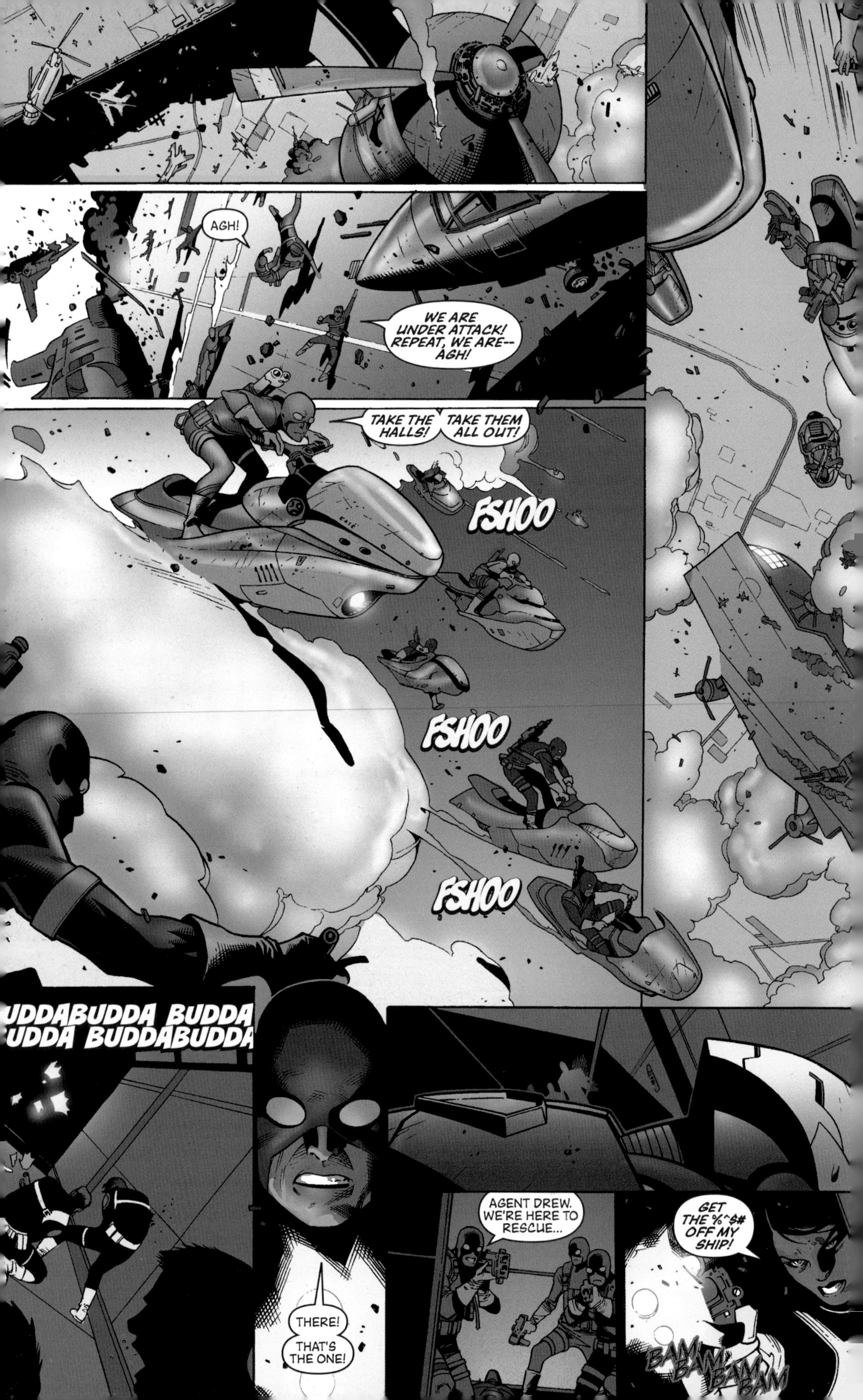
AGH!
WE ARE UNDER ATTACK! REPEAT, WE ARE-- AGH!
TAKE THE HALLS!
TAKE THEM ALL OUT!
FSHOO
FSHOO
FSHOO
UDDABUDDA BUDDA
UDDA BUDDABUDDA
THERE! THAT'S THE ONE!
AGENT DREW. WE'RE HERE TO RESCUE...
GET THE %^$# OFF MY SHIP!
BAM BAM BAM BAM

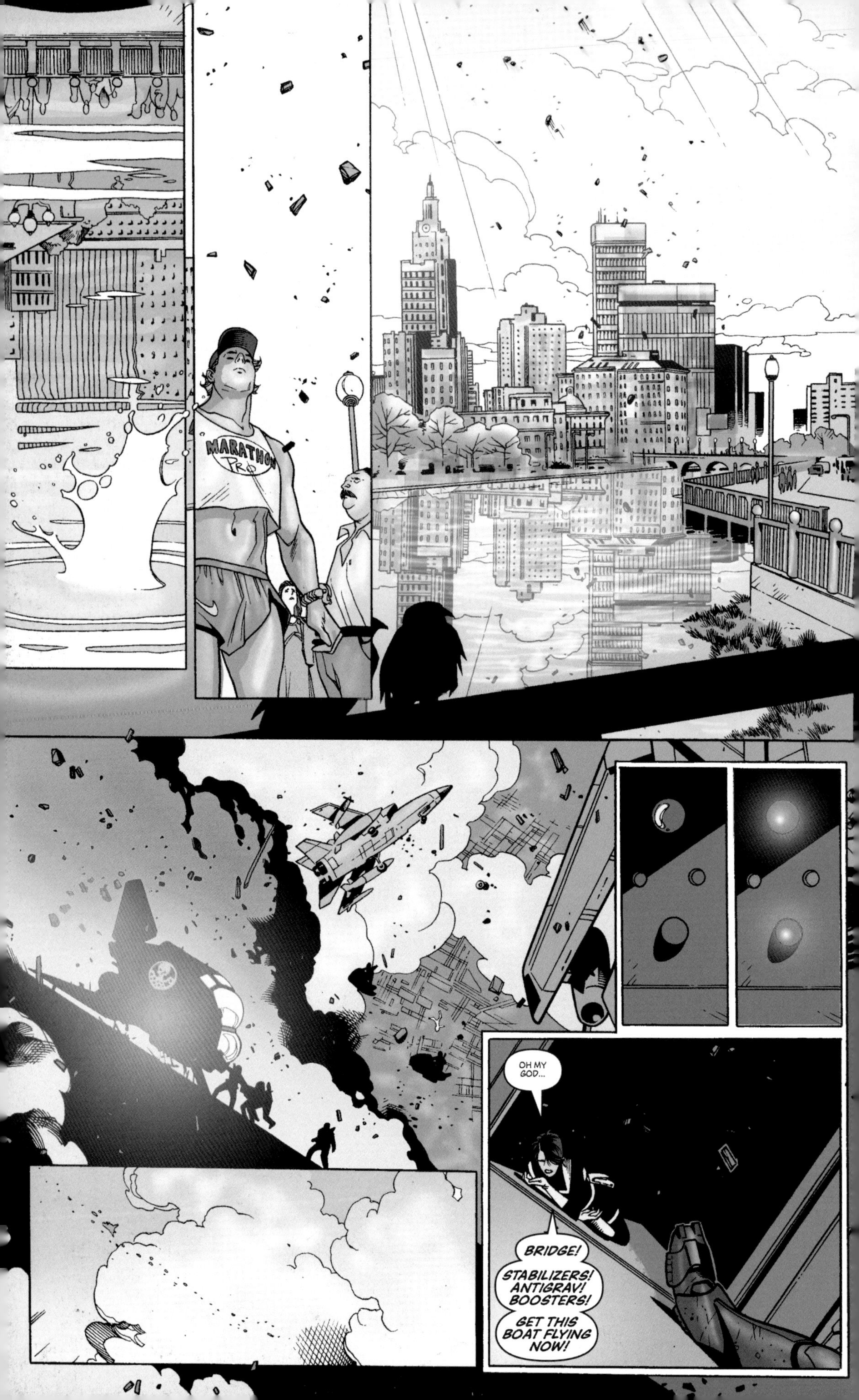
MARATHON PRO
OH MY GOD...
BRIDGE!
STABILIZERS! ANTIGRAV! BOOSTERS!
GET THIS BOAT FLYING NOW!

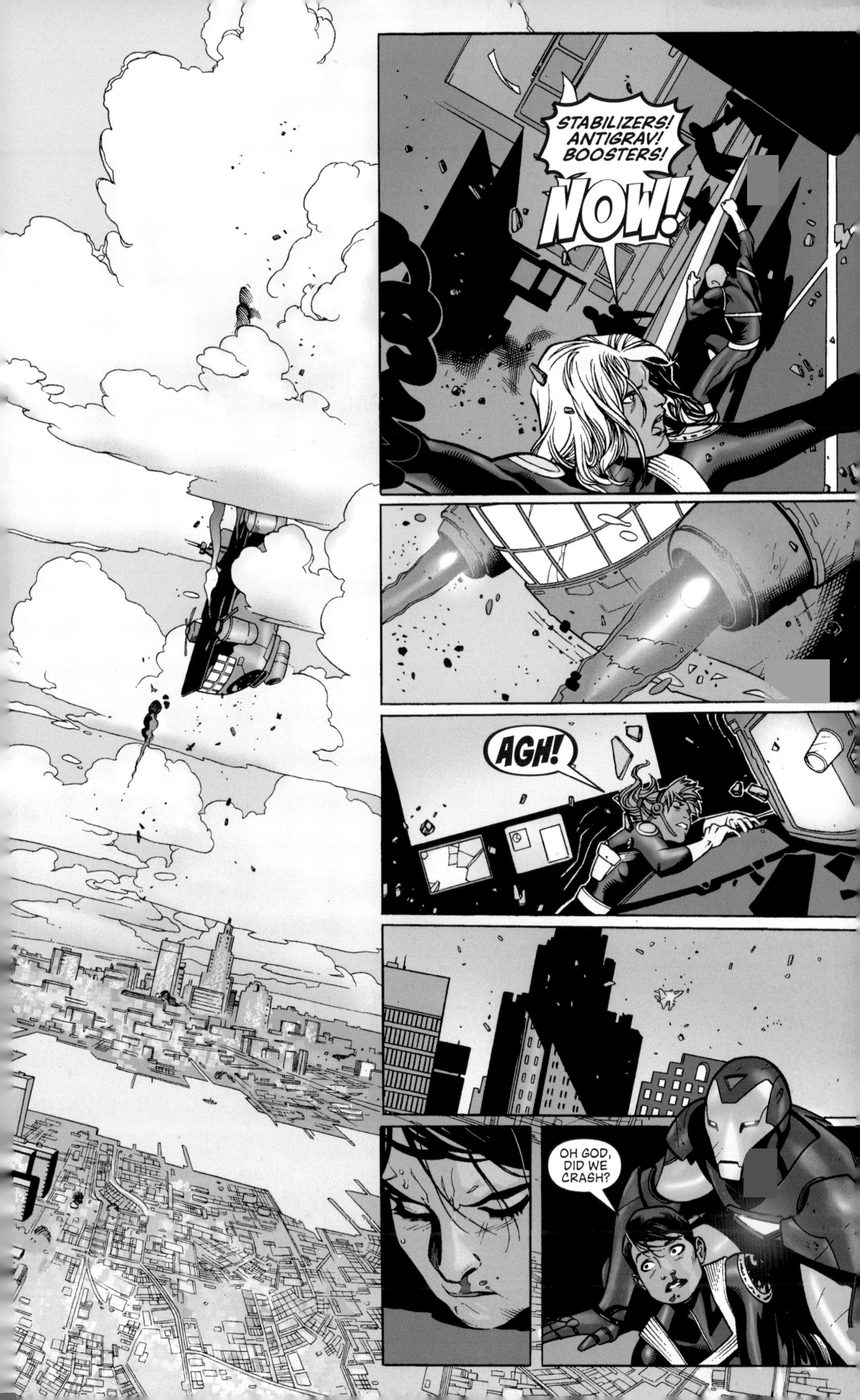
STABILIZERS! ANTIGRAV! BOOSTERS!
NOW!
AGH!
OH GOD, DID WE CRASH?

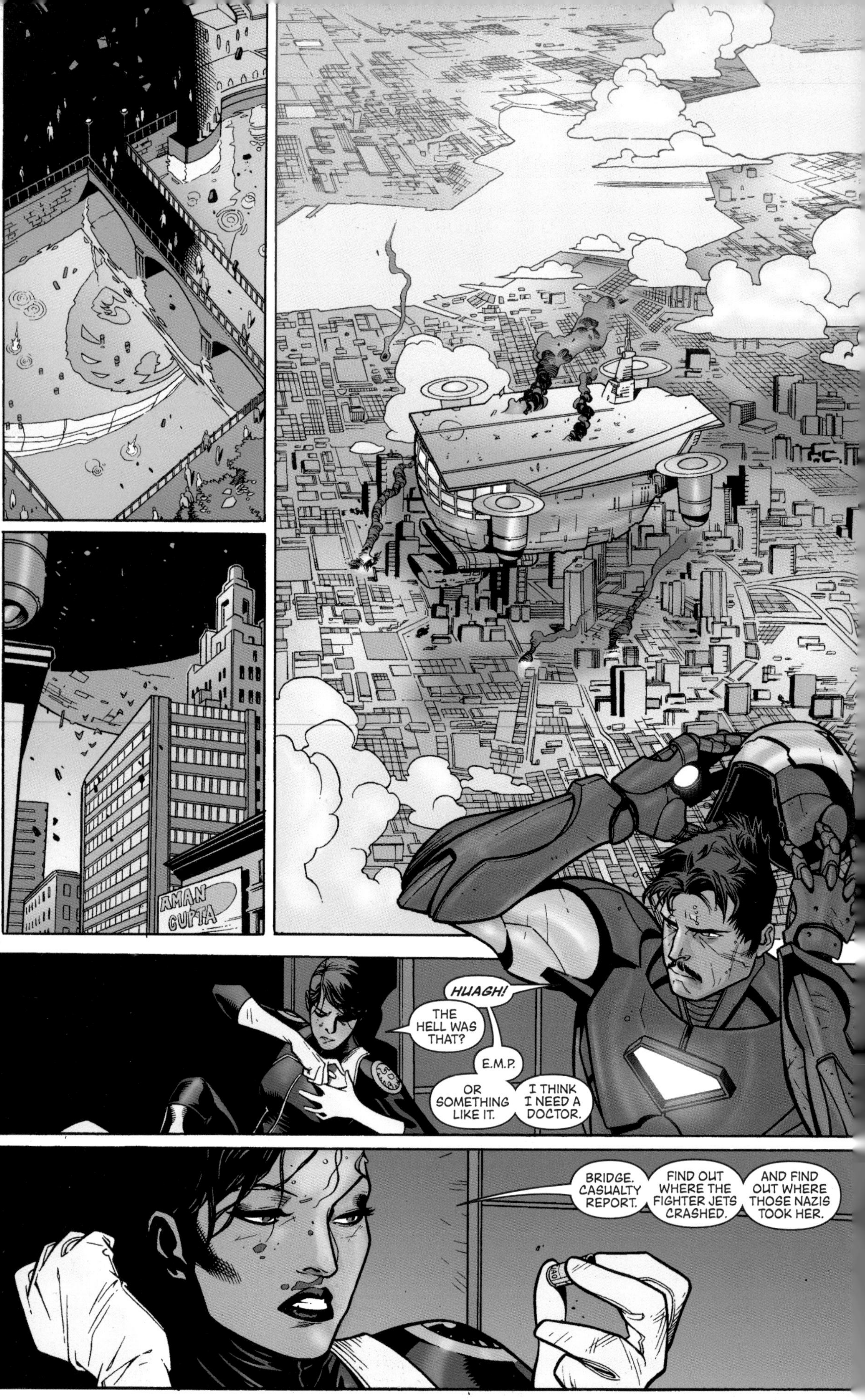
AMAN GUPTA
HUAGH!
THE HELL WAS THAT?
E.M.P.
OR SOMETHING LIKE IT.
I THINK I NEED A DOCTOR.
BRIDGE. CASUALTY REPORT.
FIND OUT WHERE THE FIGHTER JETS CRASHED.
AND FIND OUT WHERE THOSE NAZIS TOOK HER.

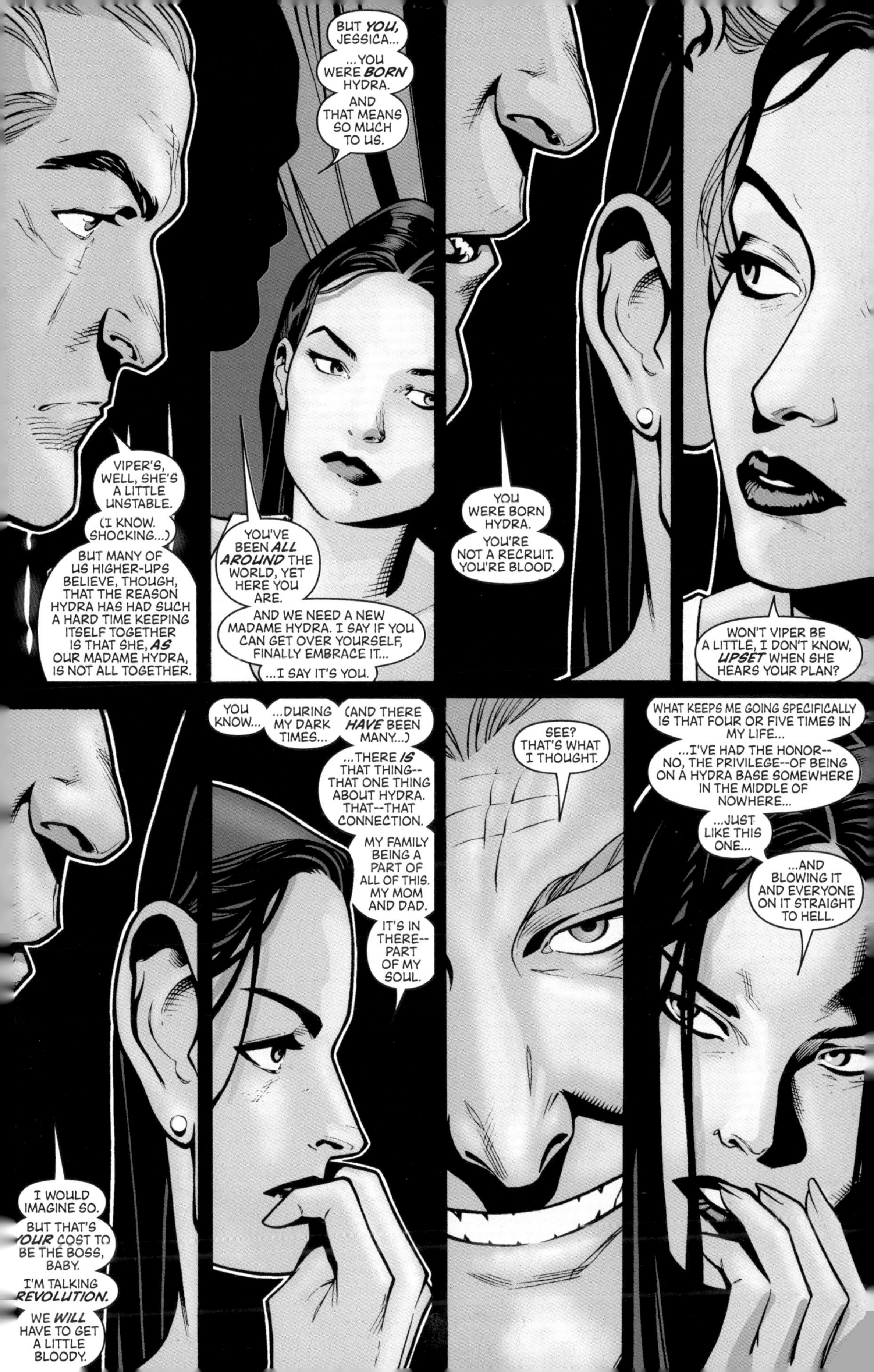
BUT YOU, JESSICA...
...YOU WERE BORN HYDRA.
AND THAT MEANS SO MUCH TO US.
VIPER'S, WELL, SHE'S A LITTLE UNSTABLE.
(I KNOW. SHOCKING...)
BUT MANY OF US HIGHER-UPS BELIEVE, THOUGH, THAT THE REASON HYDRA HAS HAD SUCH A HARD TIME KEEPING ITSELF TOGETHER IS THAT SHE, AS OUR MADAME HYDRA, IS NOT ALL TOGETHER.
YOU'VE BEEN ALL AROUND THE WORLD, YET HERE YOU ARE.
AND WE NEED A NEW MADAME HYDRA. I SAY IF YOU CAN GET OVER YOURSELF, FINALLY EMBRACE IT...
...I SAY IT'S YOU.
YOU WERE BORN HYDRA.
YOU'RE NOT A RECRUIT. YOU'RE BLOOD.
WON'T VIPER BE A LITTLE, I DON'T KNOW, UPSET WHEN SHE HEARS YOUR PLAN?
I WOULD IMAGINE SO.
BUT THAT'S YOUR COST TO BE THE BOSS, BABY.
I'M TALKING REVOLUTION.
WE WILL HAVE TO GET A LITTLE BLOODY.
YOU KNOW...
...DURING MY DARK TIMES...
(AND THERE HAVE BEEN MANY...)
...THERE IS THAT THING-- THAT ONE THING ABOUT HYDRA. THAT--THAT CONNECTION.
MY FAMILY BEING A PART OF ALL OF THIS. MY MOM AND DAD.
IT'S IN THERE-- PART OF MY SOUL.
SEE? THAT'S WHAT I THOUGHT.
WHAT KEEPS ME GOING SPECIFICALLY IS THAT FOUR OR FIVE TIMES IN MY LIFE...
...I'VE HAD THE HONOR-- NO, THE PRIVILEGE--OF BEING ON A HYDRA BASE SOMEWHERE IN THE MIDDLE OF NOWHERE...
...JUST LIKE THIS ONE...
...AND BLOWING IT AND EVERYONE ON IT STRAIGHT TO HELL.

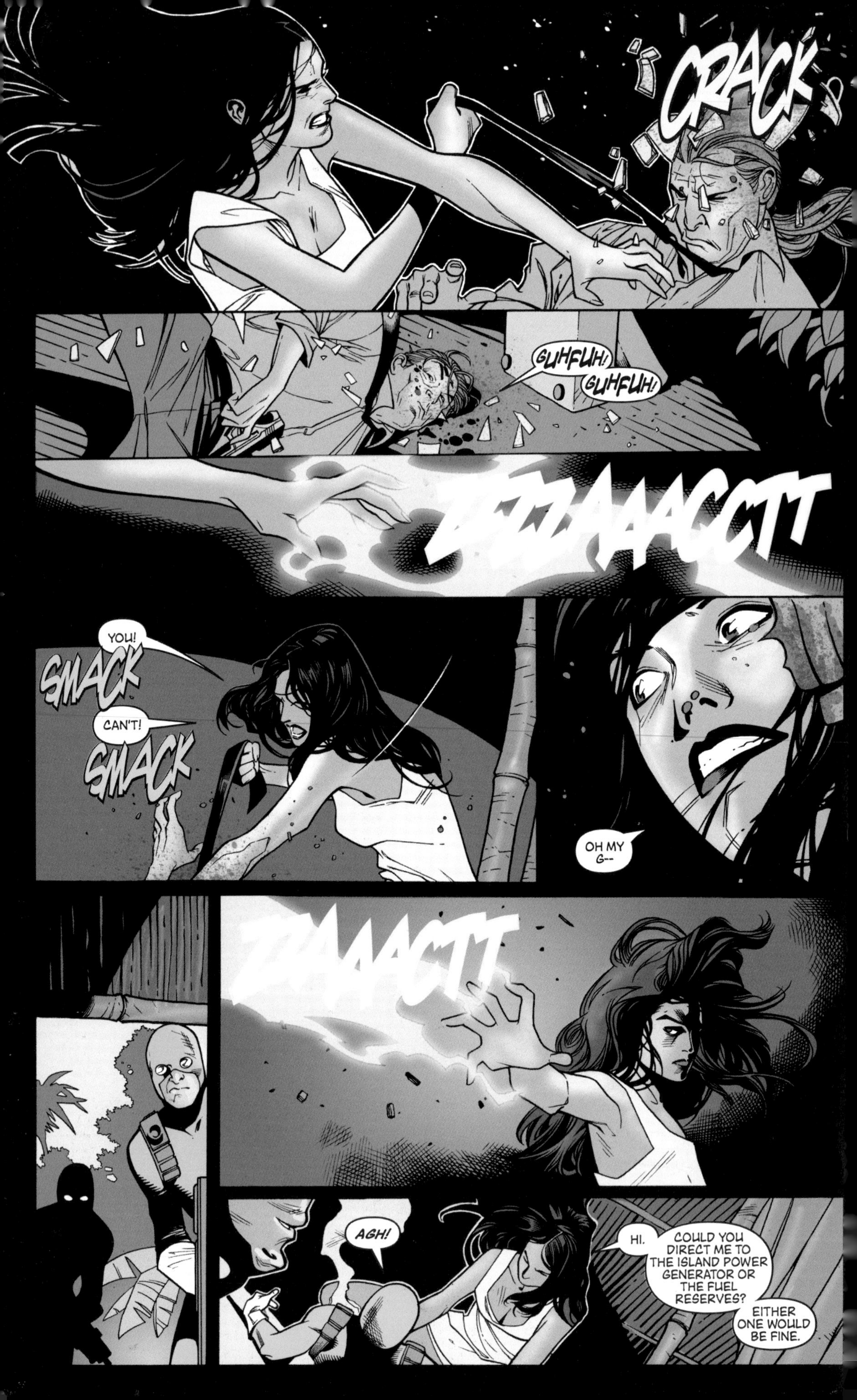
CRACK
GUHFUH!
GUHFUH!
ZZZAAACCTT
YOU!
SMACK
CAN'T!
SMACK
OH MY G--
ZZAAACTT
AGH!
HI.
COULD YOU DIRECT ME TO THE ISLAND POWER GENERATOR OR THE FUEL RESERVES?
EITHER ONE WOULD BE FINE.

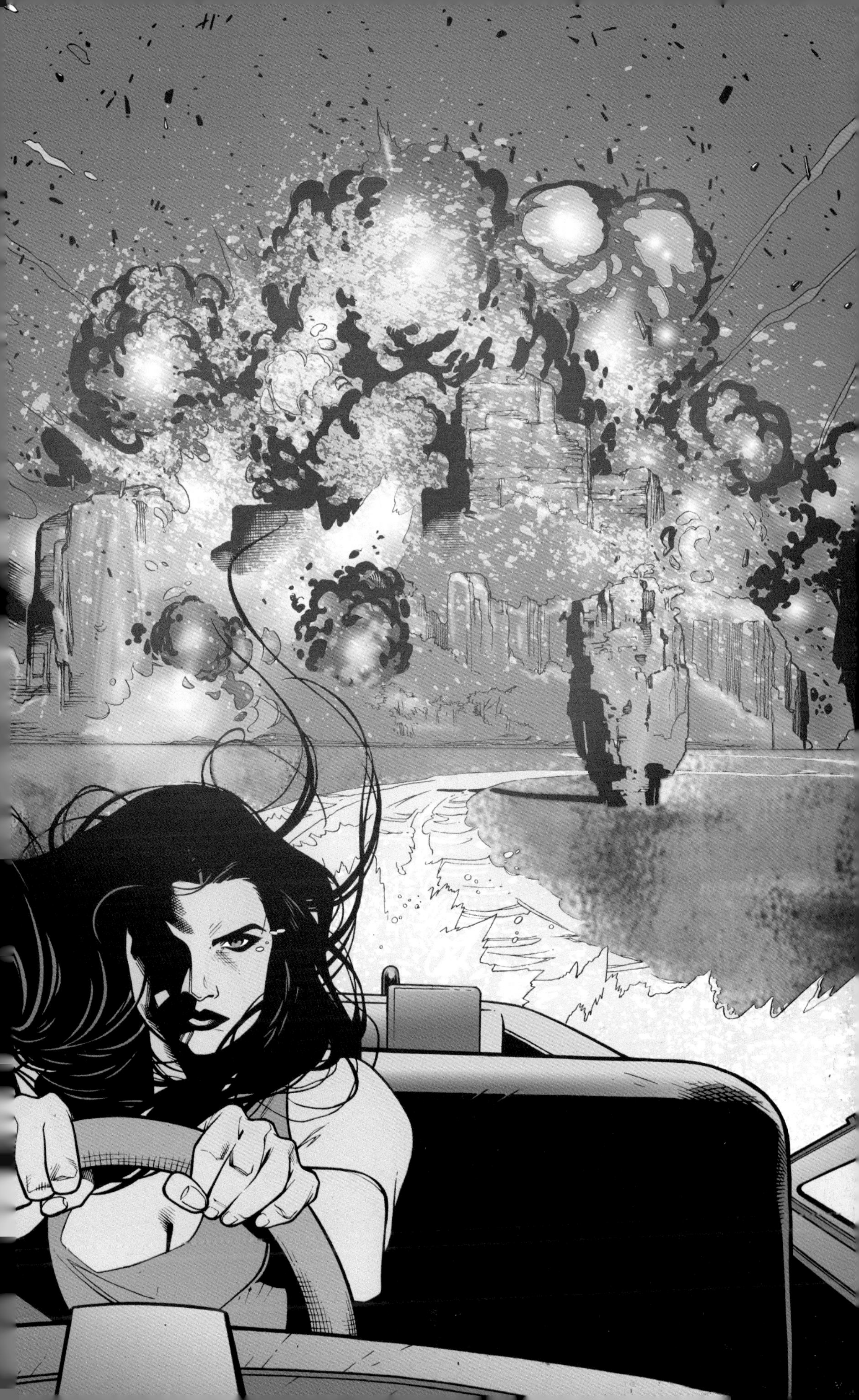

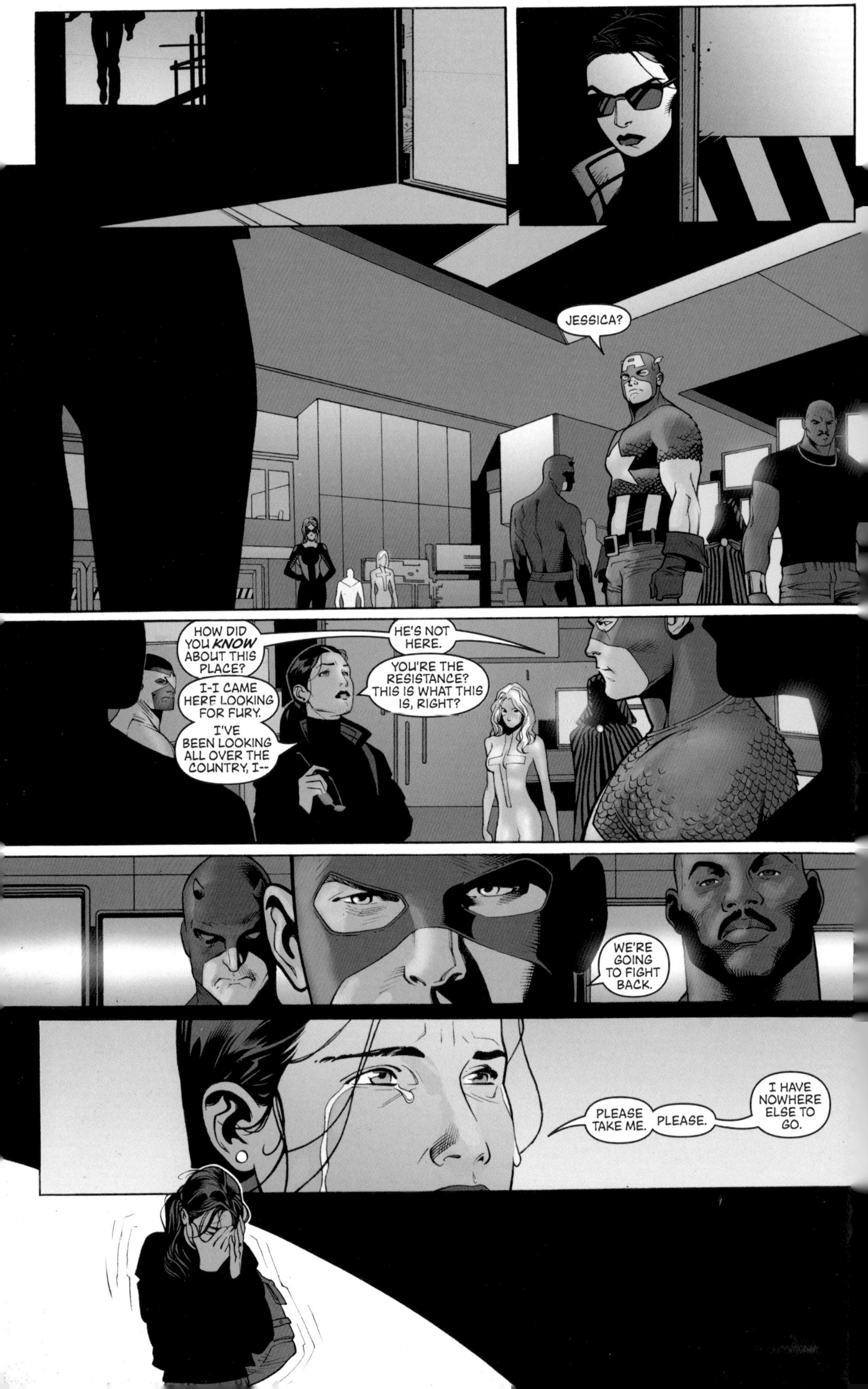
JESSICA?
HOW DID YOU *KNOW* ABOUT THIS PLACE?
HE'S NOT HERE.
I-I CAME HERE LOOKING FOR FURY.
I'VE BEEN LOOKING ALL OVER THE COUNTRY, I--
YOU'RE THE RESISTANCE? THIS IS WHAT THIS IS, RIGHT?
WE'RE GOING TO FIGHT BACK.
PLEASE TAKE ME.
PLEASE.
I HAVE NOWHERE ELSE TO GO.

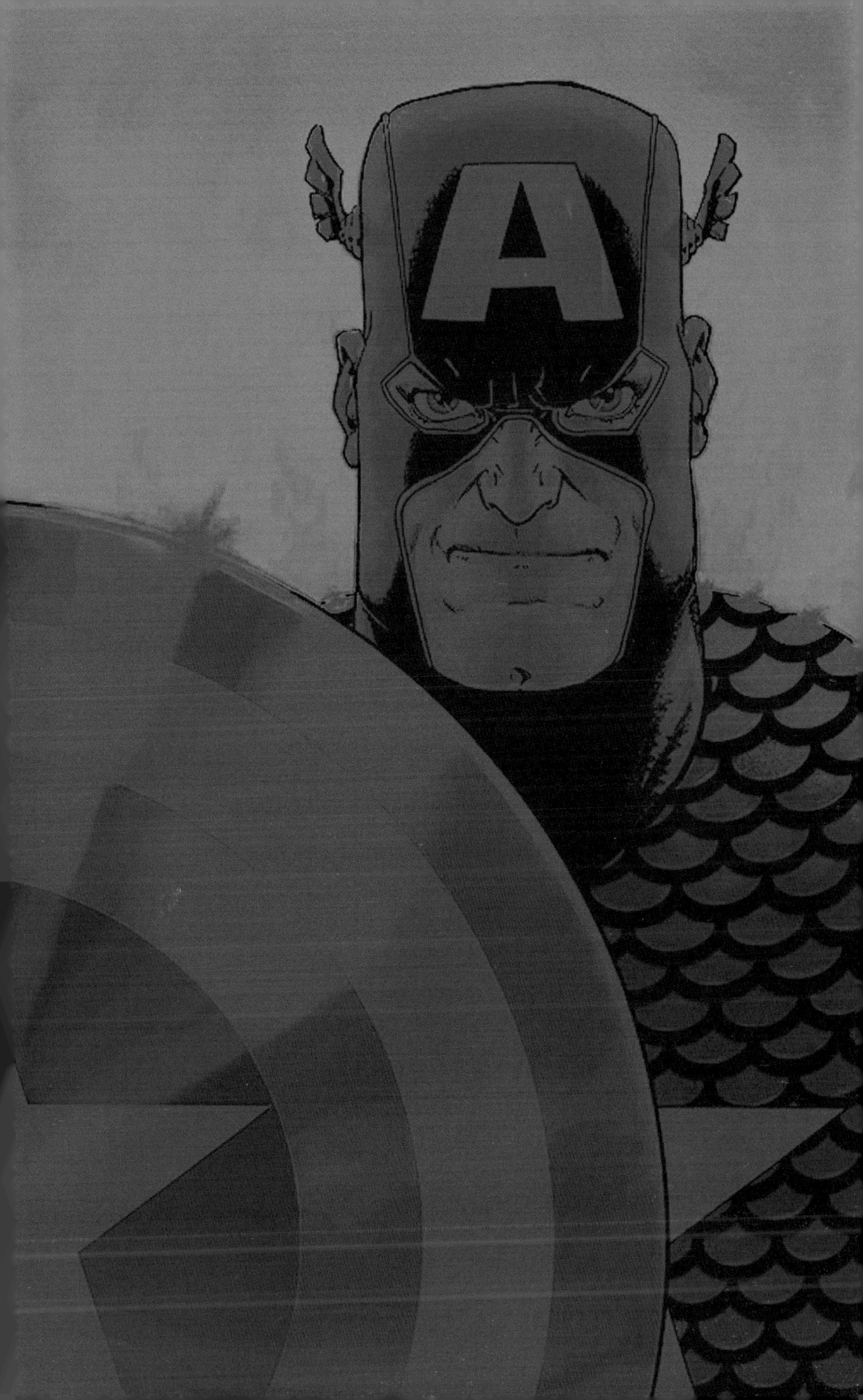

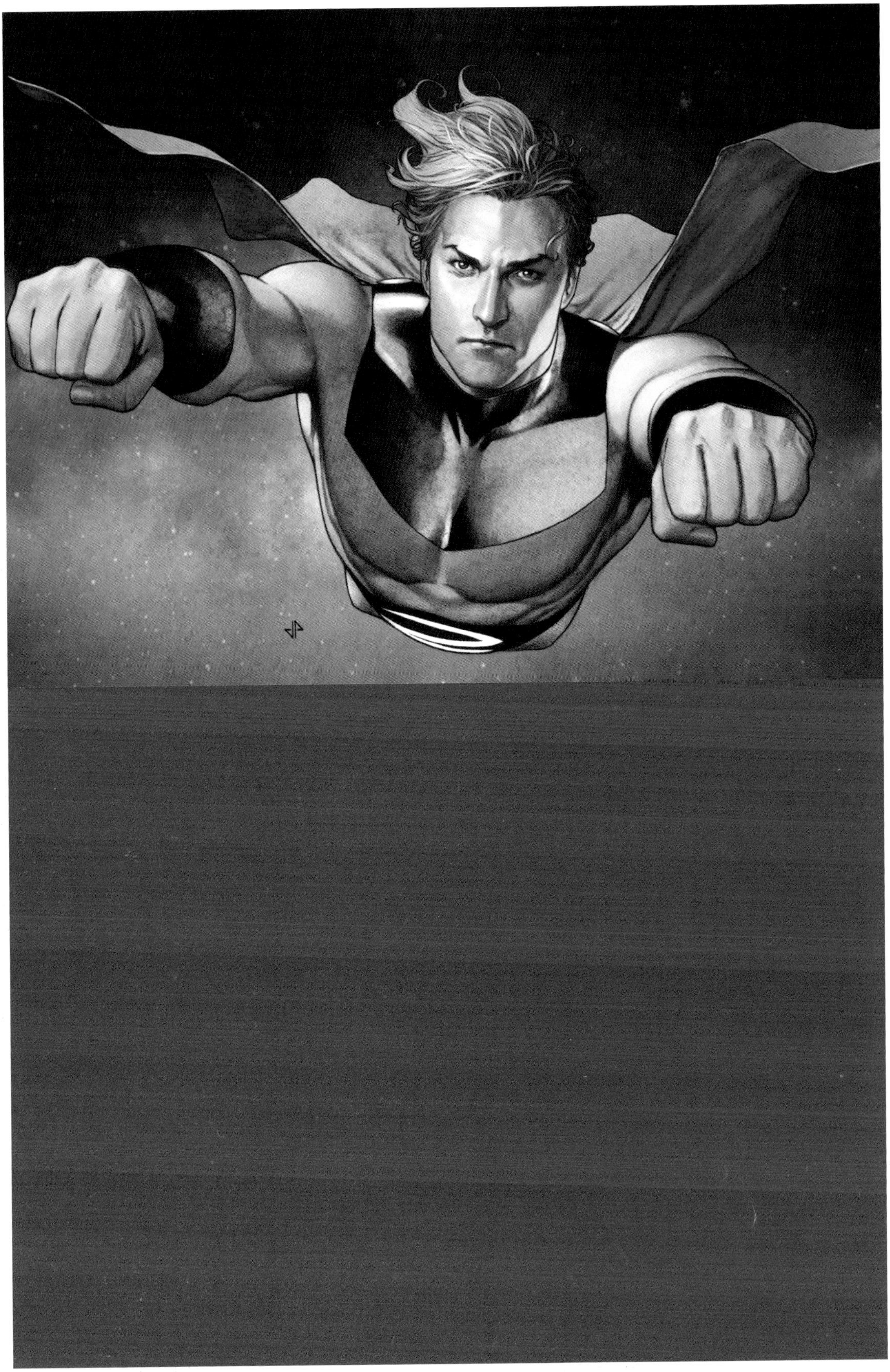

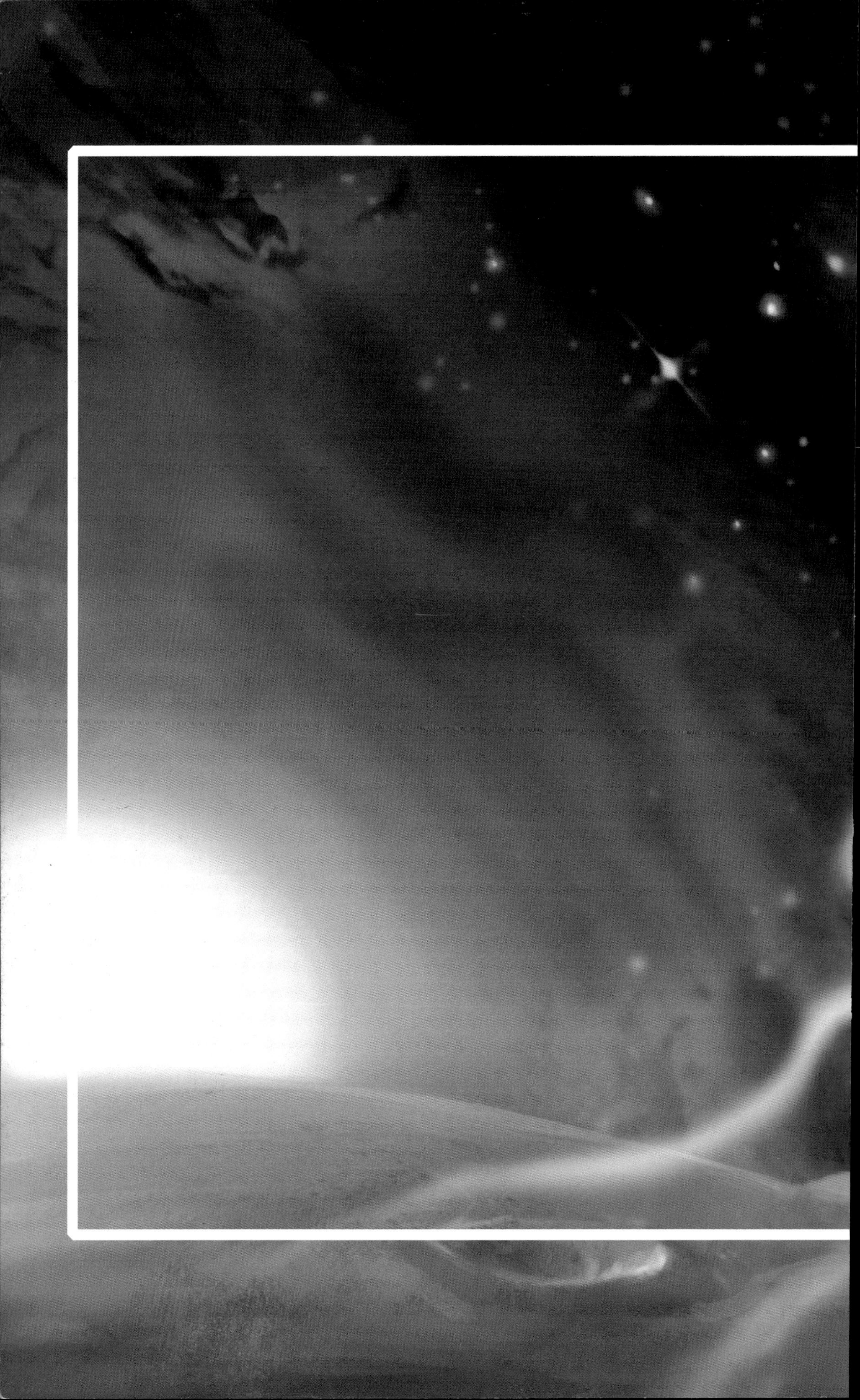

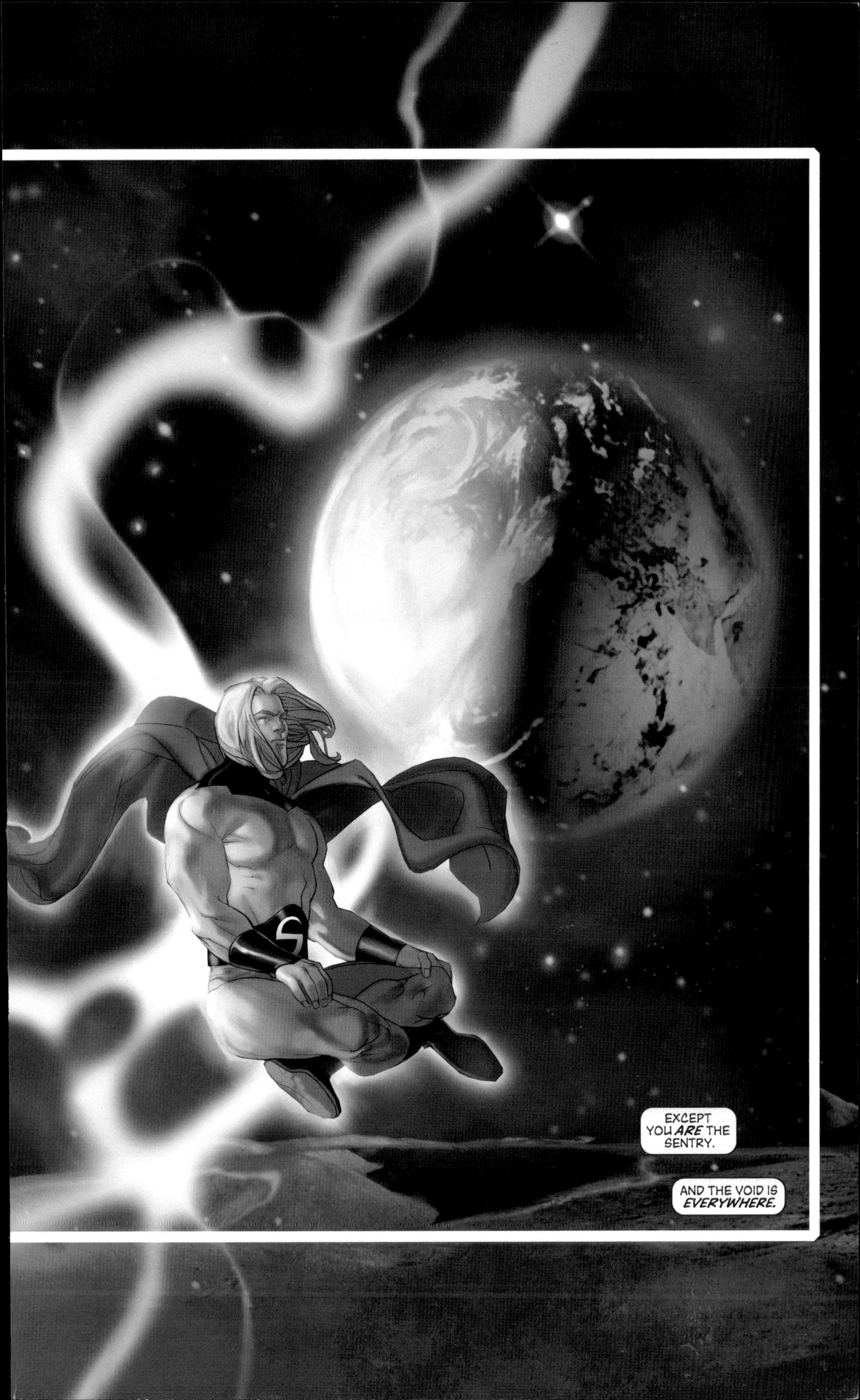
EXCEPT YOU *ARE* THE SENTRY.
AND THE VOID IS *EVERYWHERE.*

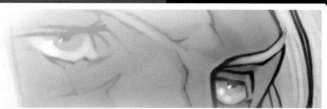

STOP TALKING ABOUT THE VOID WHEN IT'S *YOU* THAT'S THE PROBLEM.

STOP WALLOWING. EVERYONE HAS PROBLEMS.

EXCEPT YOU RAN *AWAY* FROM YOURS.

WHAT KIND OF HERO *ARE* YOU, BOB?

YOU SHOULD GO *BACK THERE* AND USE YOUR POWER TO MOLD THE WORLD INTO WHAT YOU *KNOW* IT SHOULD BE.

YOU HAVE THE POWER TO *STOP* THIS ENTIRE WAR!

YOU HAVE THE POWER TO COMPLETELY REMOVE IT FROM THE HISTORY BOOKS.

YOU COULD GO THERE AND-- WHAT? *WHAT?*

WHAT WOULD YOU DO, BOB?

AND WHAT WOULD BE YOUR--

THE INHUMANS.

YOU KNOW THEM.

RIGHT?

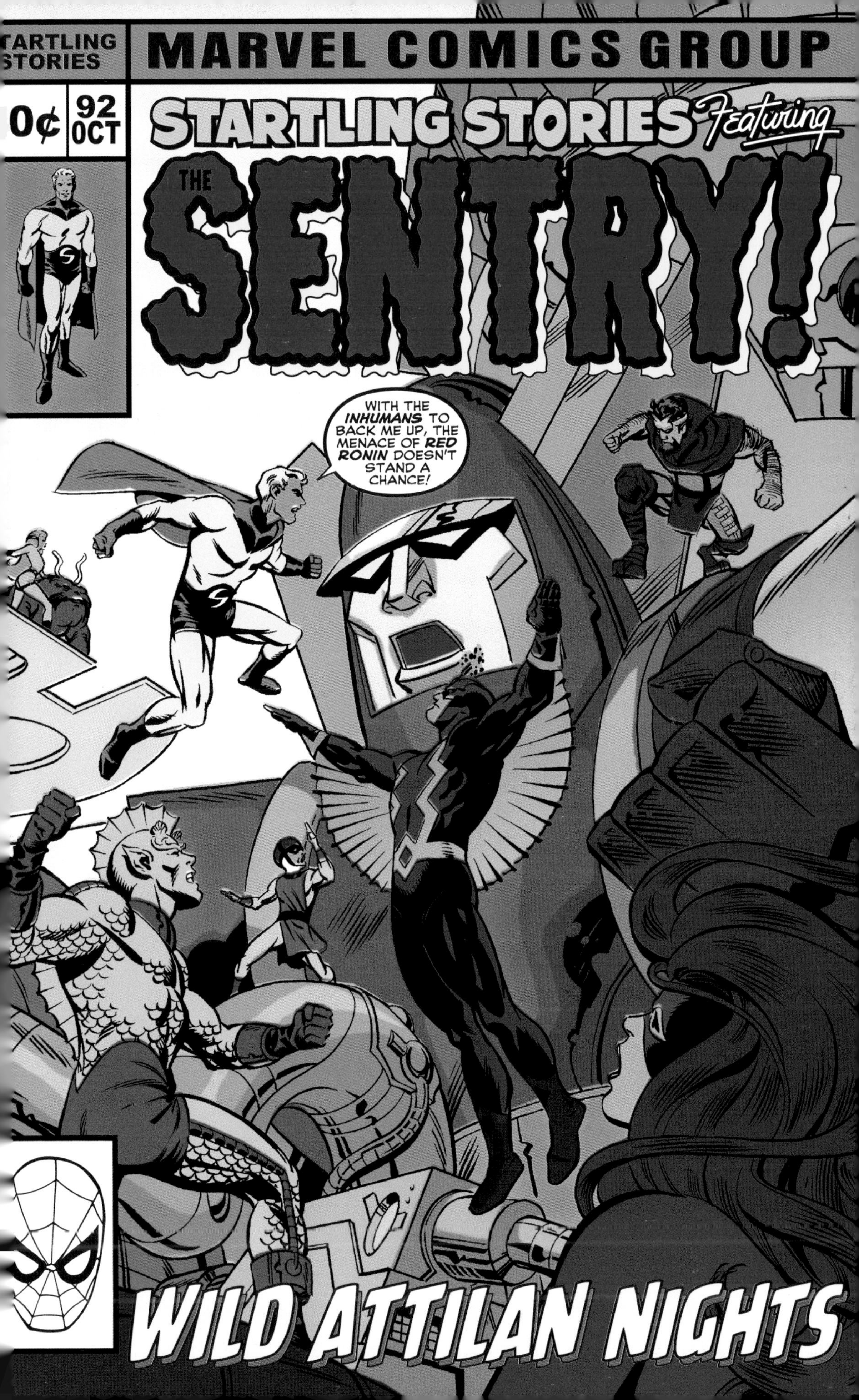
STARTLING STORIES
MARVEL COMICS GROUP
0¢
92 OCT
STARTLING STORIES Featuring
THE SENTRY!
WITH THE INHUMANS TO BACK ME UP, THE MENACE OF RED RONIN DOESN'T STAND A CHANCE!
WILD ATTILAN NIGHTS

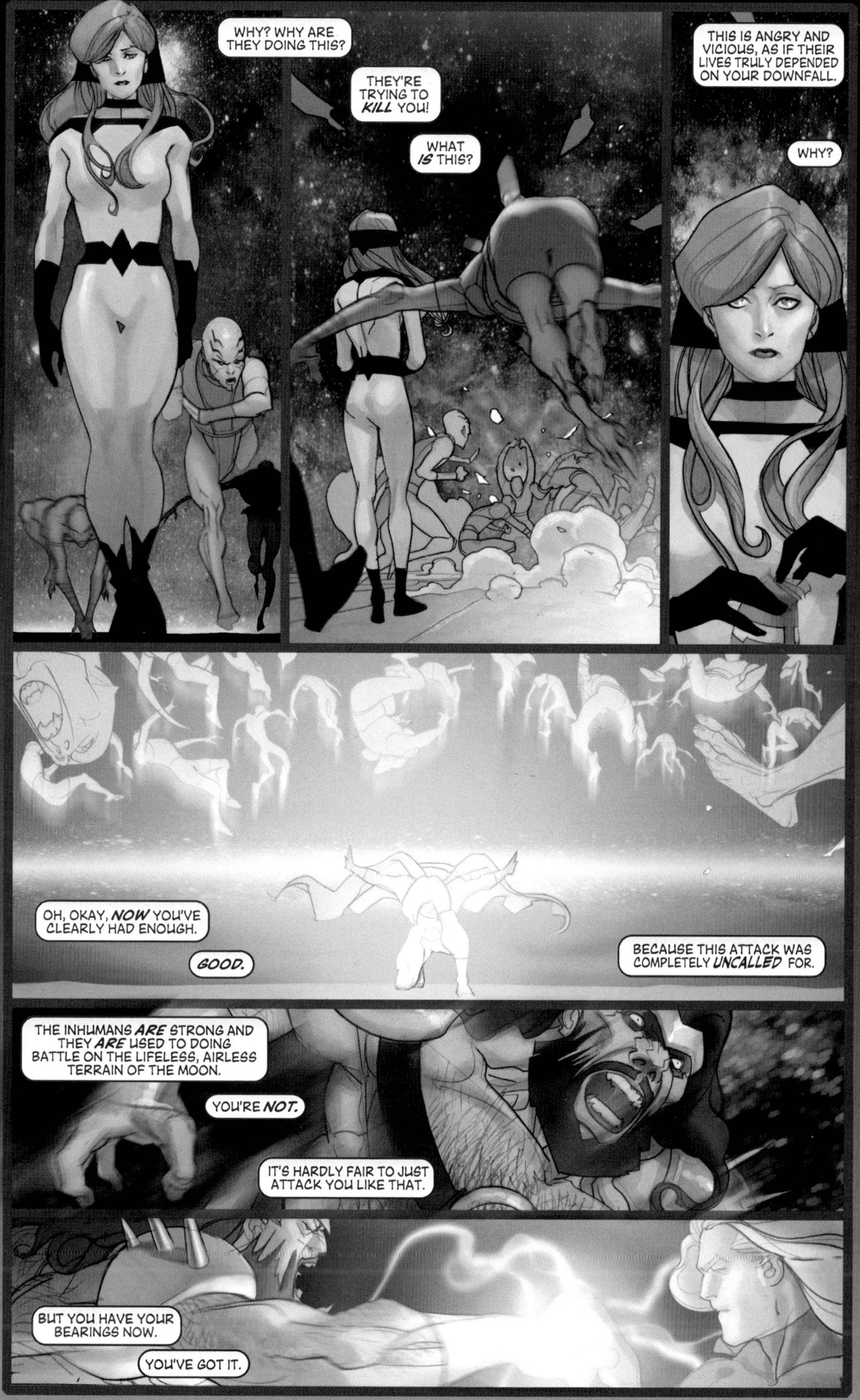
WHY? WHY ARE THEY DOING THIS?
THEY'RE TRYING TO *KILL* YOU!
WHAT *IS* THIS?
THIS IS ANGRY AND VICIOUS, AS IF THEIR LIVES TRULY DEPENDED ON YOUR DOWNFALL.
WHY?
OH, OKAY, *NOW* YOU'VE CLEARLY HAD ENOUGH.
GOOD.
BECAUSE THIS ATTACK WAS COMPLETELY *UNCALLED* FOR.
THE INHUMANS *ARE* STRONG AND THEY *ARE* USED TO DOING BATTLE ON THE LIFELESS, AIRLESS TERRAIN OF THE MOON.
YOU'RE *NOT.*
IT'S HARDLY FAIR TO JUST ATTACK YOU LIKE THAT.
BUT YOU HAVE YOUR BEARINGS NOW.
YOU'VE GOT IT.

YOU HOLD THEM AND DON'T FIGHT THEM.

MAYBE THAT WILL SEND THE VOICELESS MESSAGE THAT YOU *COULD* FIGHT BACK BUT *CHOOSE* NOT TO.

VERY MATURE OF YOU, BOB. GOOD FOR YOU.

THE ENTIRE REASON YOU CAME ALL THE WAY OUT HERE IS SO YOU COULD THINK OF SOMETHING TO DO *OTHER* THAN FIGHTING POINTLESSLY AGAINST FRIENDS AND ALLIES.

THE FIGHT IS OVER BECAUSE *YOU* SAY IT IS.

BUT WHAT ARE YOU DOING, BOB? YOU COULD EASILY BREAK THEM--OH.

YOU'RE JUST GOING TO *HOLD* THEM.

THEY ARE JUST GOING TO HAVE TO FIGURE OUT ANOTHER WAY TO COMMUNICATE TO YOU EXACTLY WHAT THEIR *PROBLEM* IS.

BUT WHY DON'T YOU JUST FLY AWAY, BOB?

JUST LEAVE THEM WITH THEIR ANGER AND--

BLACK BOLT'S HEADDRESS?

AT FIRST YOU DON'T UNDERSTAND THE GESTURE.

THE INHUMANS HAVE THEIR OWN CUSTOMS.

BUT THEN YOU REALIZE... IT'S A SUMMONS.

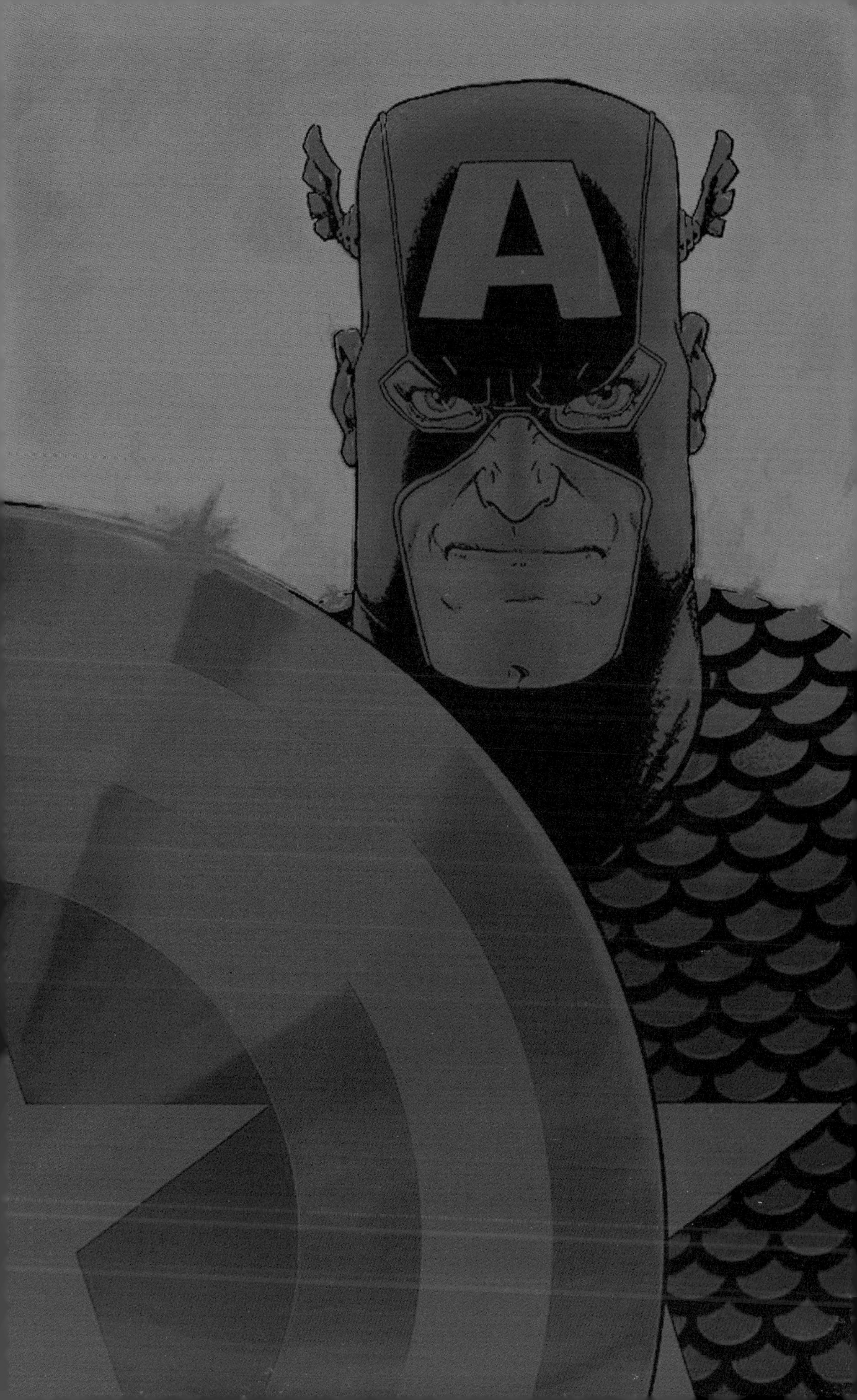

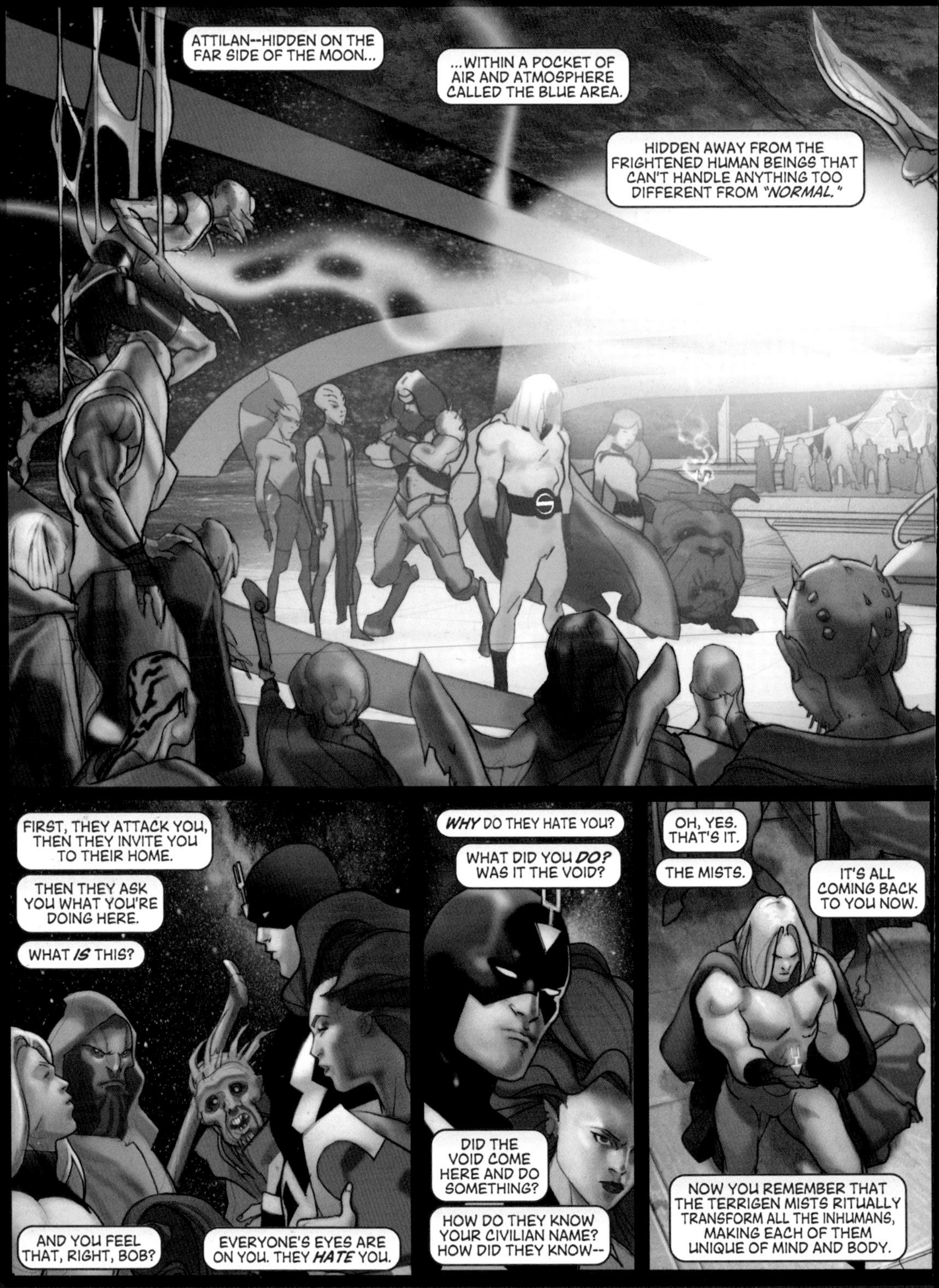
ATTILAN--HIDDEN ON THE FAR SIDE OF THE MOON...
...WITHIN A POCKET OF AIR AND ATMOSPHERE CALLED THE BLUE AREA.
HIDDEN AWAY FROM THE FRIGHTENED HUMAN BEINGS THAT CAN'T HANDLE ANYTHING TOO DIFFERENT FROM "NORMAL."
FIRST, THEY ATTACK YOU, THEN THEY INVITE YOU TO THEIR HOME.
THEN THEY ASK YOU WHAT YOU'RE DOING HERE.
WHAT IS THIS?
AND YOU FEEL THAT, RIGHT, BOB?
EVERYONE'S EYES ARE ON YOU. THEY HATE YOU.
WHY DO THEY HATE YOU?
WHAT DID YOU DO? WAS IT THE VOID?
DID THE VOID COME HERE AND DO SOMETHING?
HOW DO THEY KNOW YOUR CIVILIAN NAME? HOW DID THEY KNOW--
OH, YES. THAT'S IT.
THE MISTS.
IT'S ALL COMING BACK TO YOU NOW.
NOW YOU REMEMBER THAT THE TERRIGEN MISTS RITUALLY TRANSFORM ALL THE INHUMANS, MAKING EACH OF THEM UNIQUE OF MIND AND BODY.

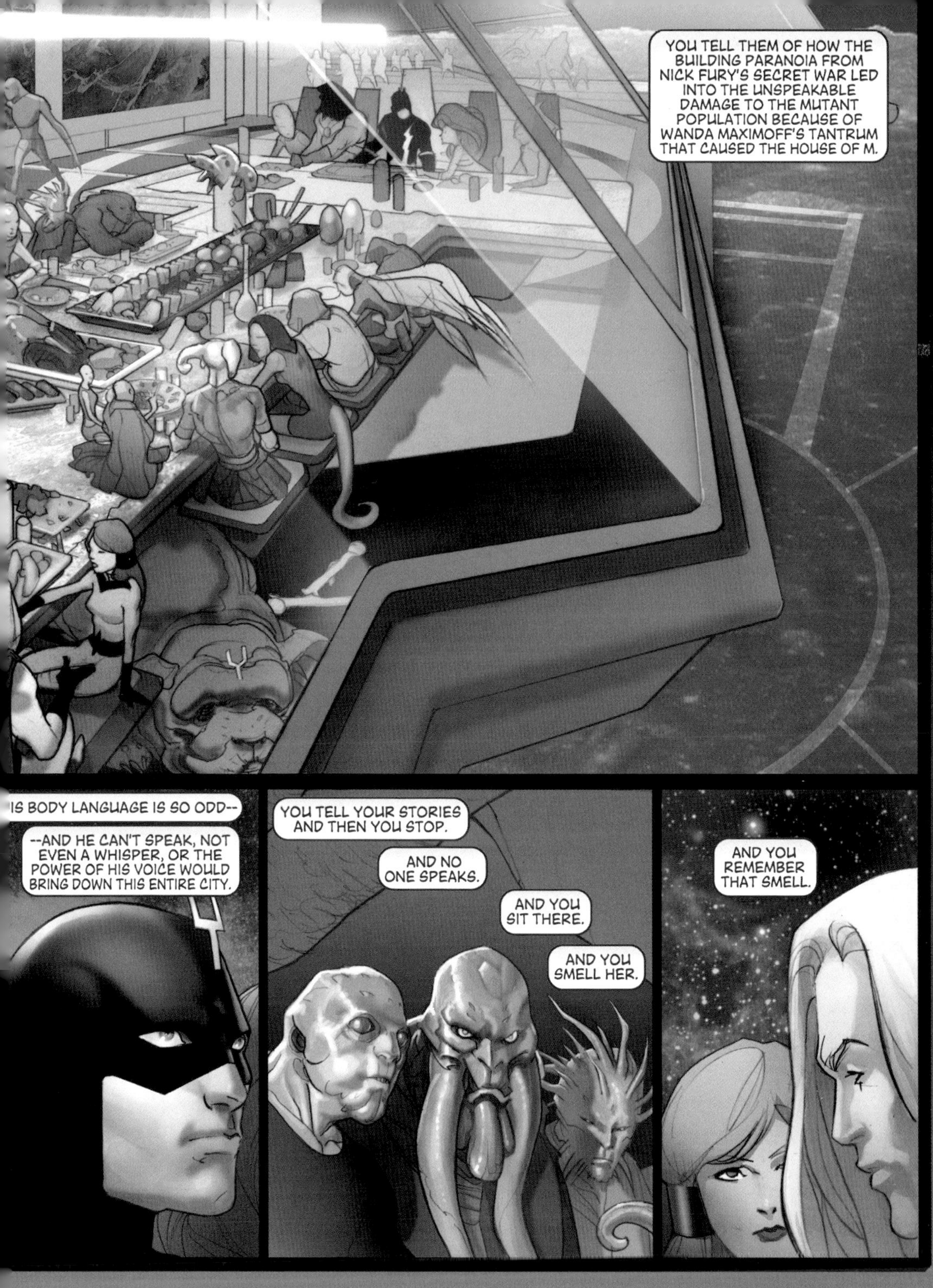
YOU TELL THEM OF HOW THE BUILDING PARANOIA FROM NICK FURY'S SECRET WAR LED INTO THE UNSPEAKABLE DAMAGE TO THE MUTANT POPULATION BECAUSE OF WANDA MAXIMOFF'S TANTRUM THAT CAUSED THE HOUSE OF M.
IS BODY LANGUAGE IS SO ODD--
--AND HE CAN'T SPEAK, NOT EVEN A WHISPER, OR THE POWER OF HIS VOICE WOULD BRING DOWN THIS ENTIRE CITY.
YOU TELL YOUR STORIES AND THEN YOU STOP.
AND NO ONE SPEAKS.
AND YOU SIT THERE.
AND YOU SMELL HER.
AND YOU REMEMBER THAT SMELL.

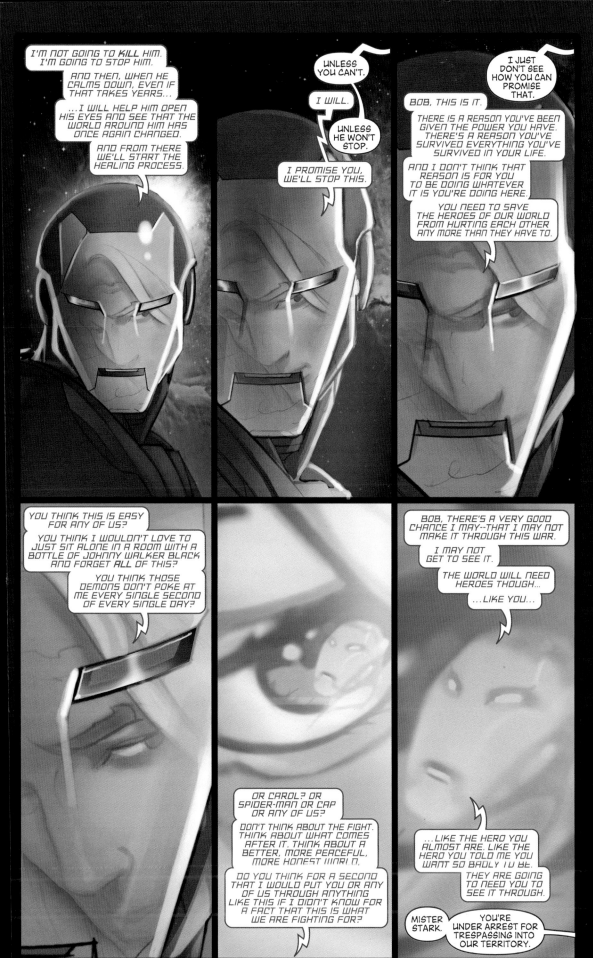

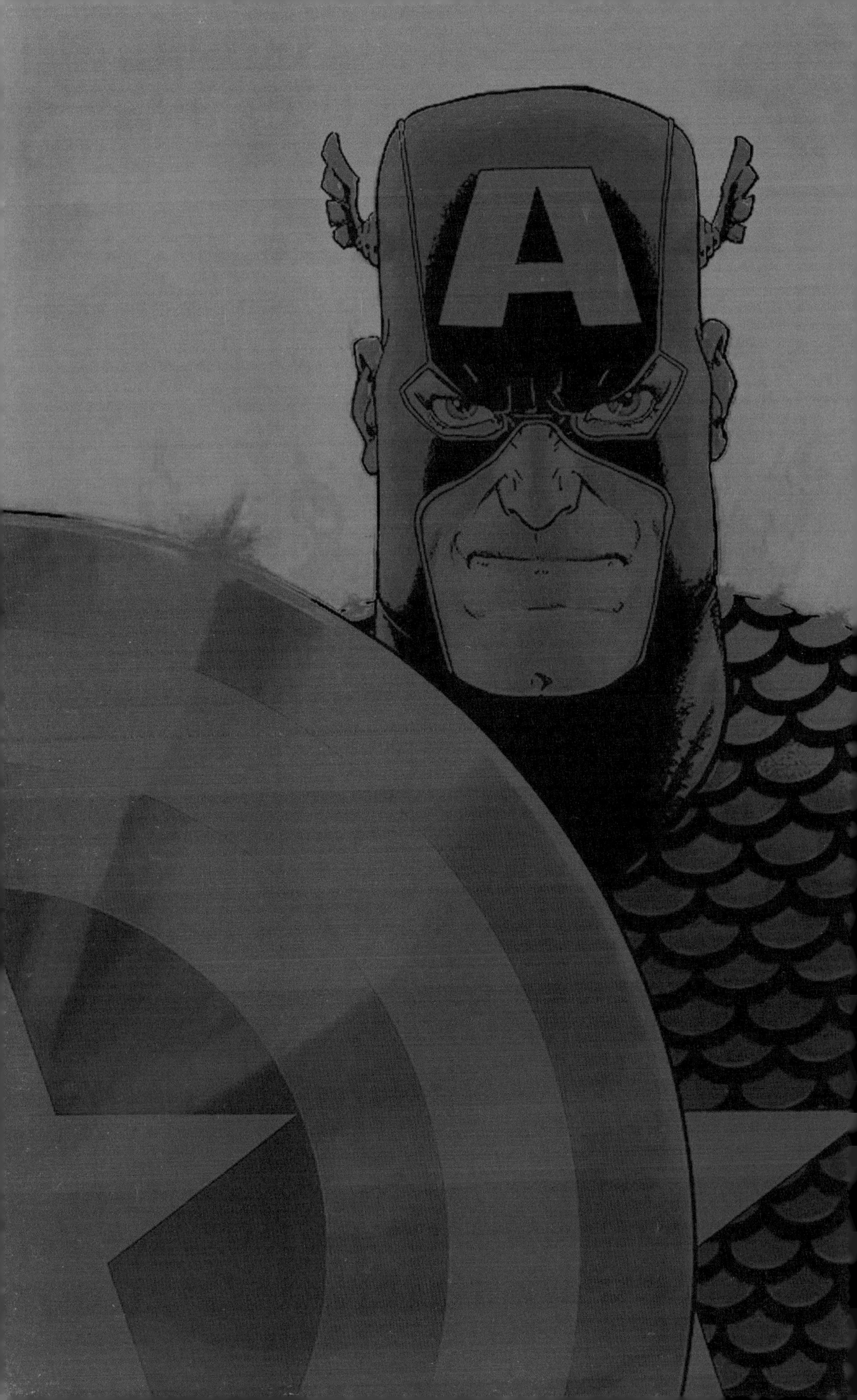

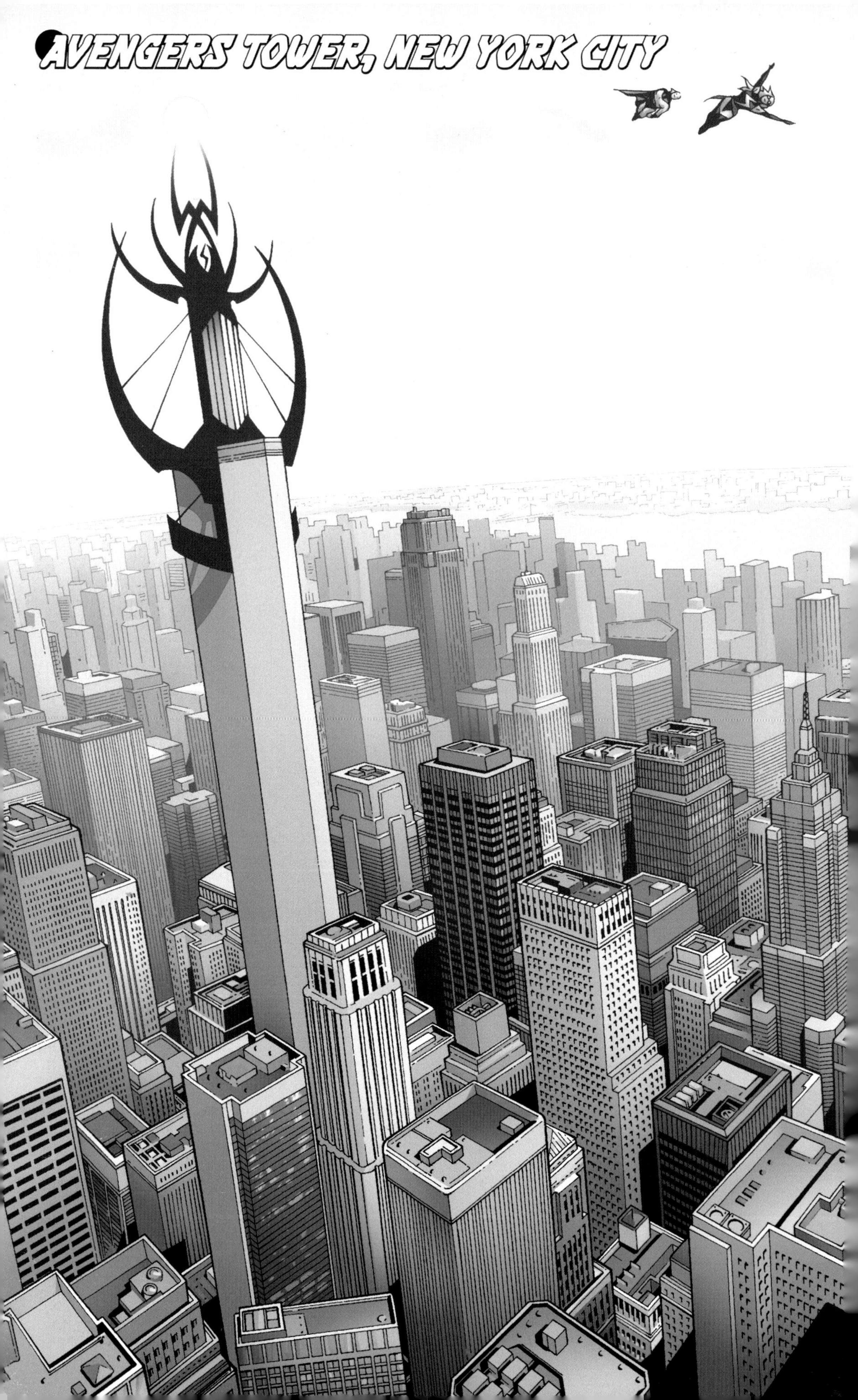
AVENGERS TOWER, NEW YORK CITY

CLANG CLLNG

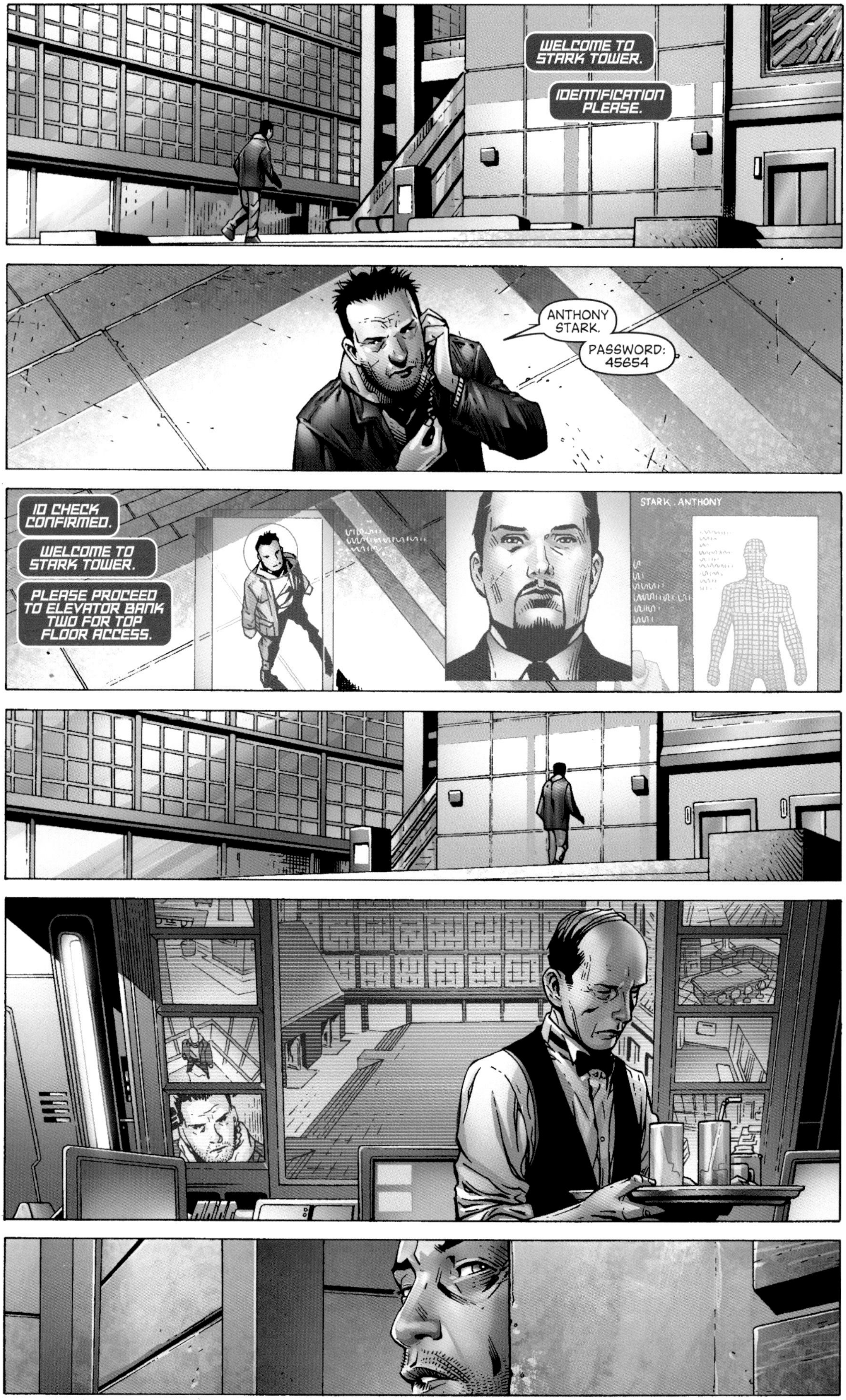
WELCOME TO STARK TOWER.
IDENTIFICATION PLEASE.
ANTHONY STARK.
PASSWORD: 45654
ID CHECK CONFIRMED.
WELCOME TO STARK TOWER.
PLEASE PROCEED TO ELEVATOR BANK TWO FOR TOP FLOOR ACCESS.
STARK . ANTHONY

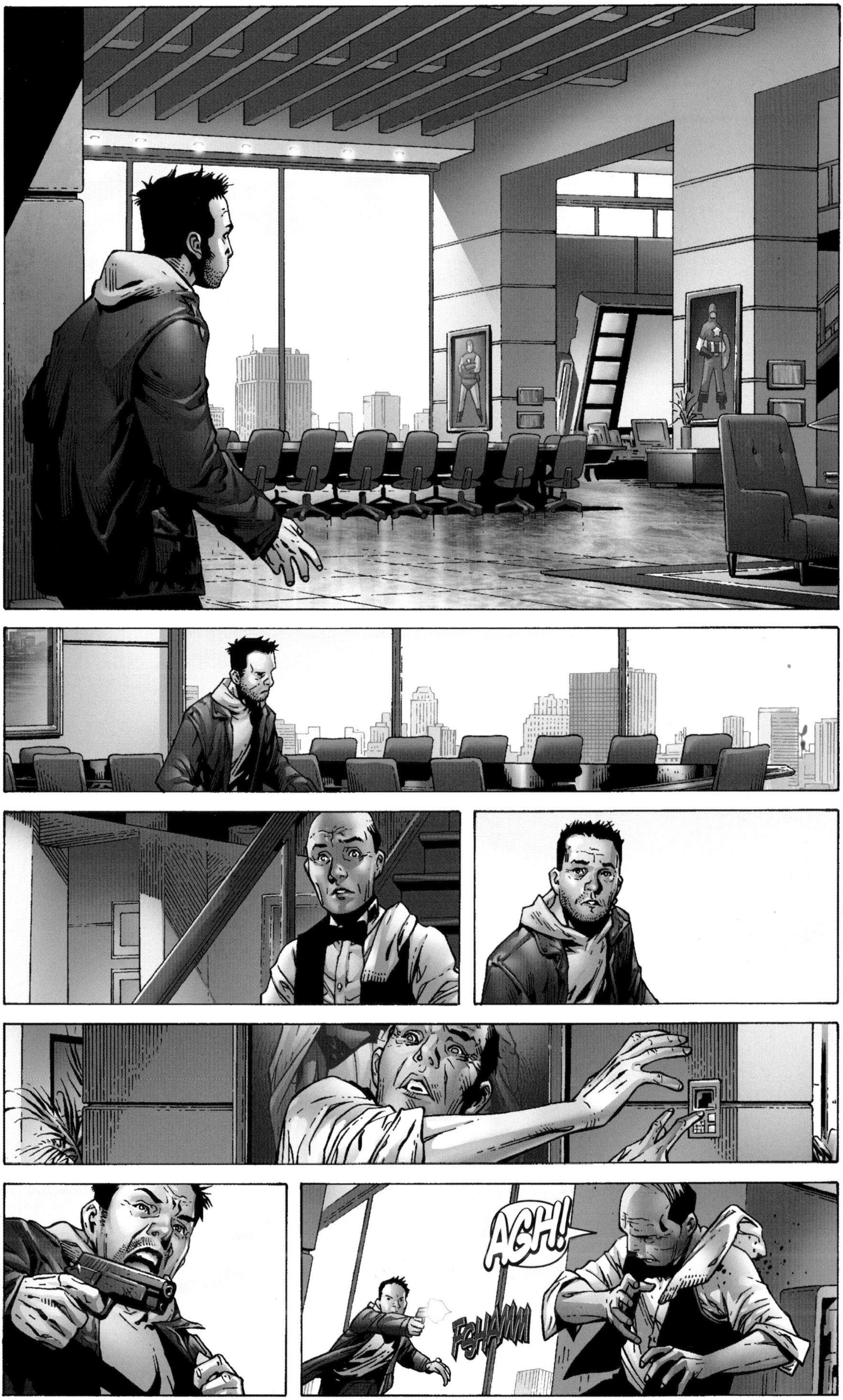

AGH!
FSHAMM

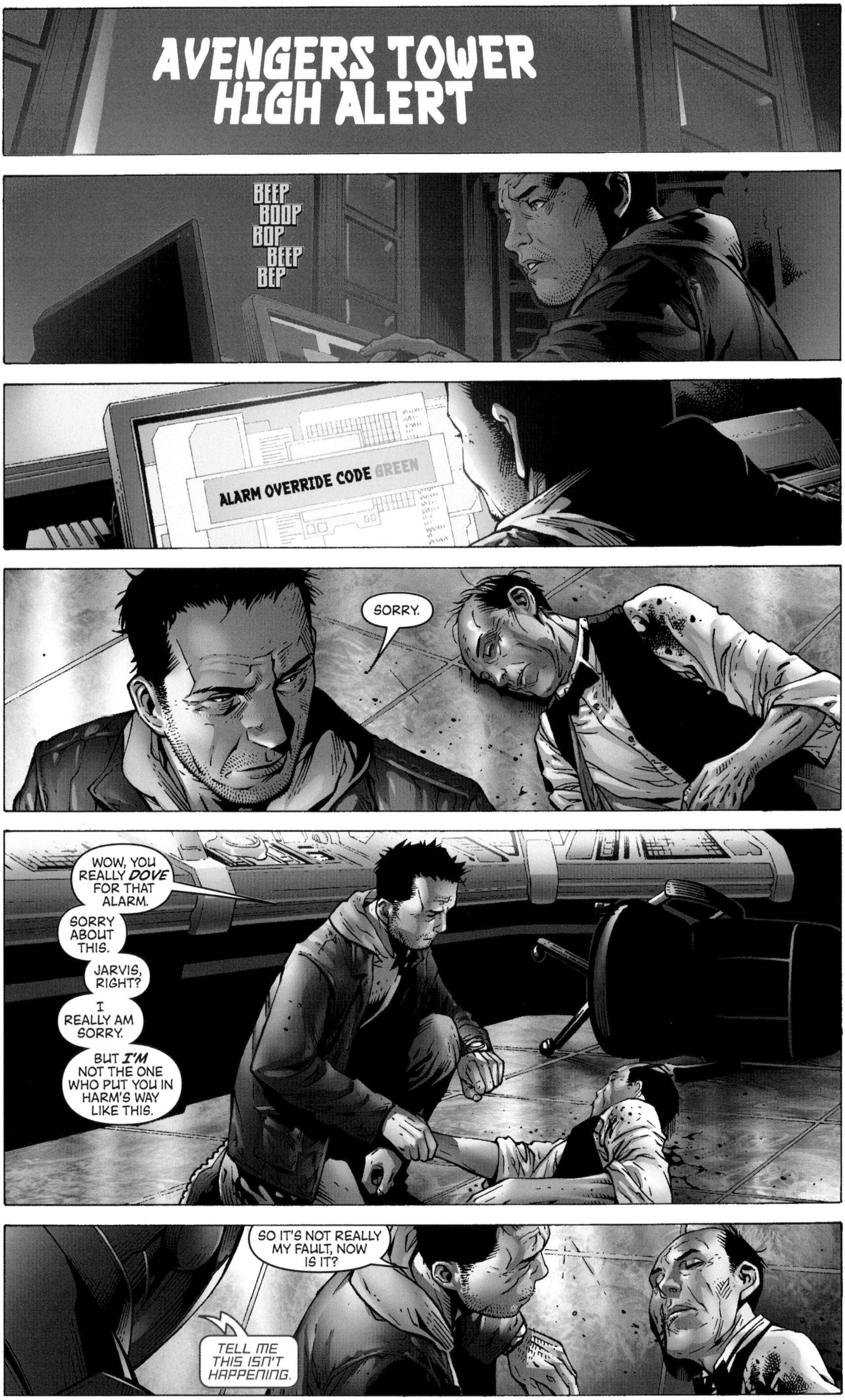
AVENGERS TOWER
HIGH ALERT
BEEP BOOP BOP BEEP BEP
ALARM OVERRIDE CODE GREEN
SORRY.
WOW, YOU REALLY *DOVE* FOR THAT ALARM.
SORRY ABOUT THIS.
JARVIS, RIGHT?
I REALLY AM SORRY.
BUT *I'M* NOT THE ONE WHO PUT YOU IN HARM'S WAY LIKE THIS.
SO IT'S NOT REALLY MY FAULT, NOW IS IT?
TELL ME THIS ISN'T HAPPENING.

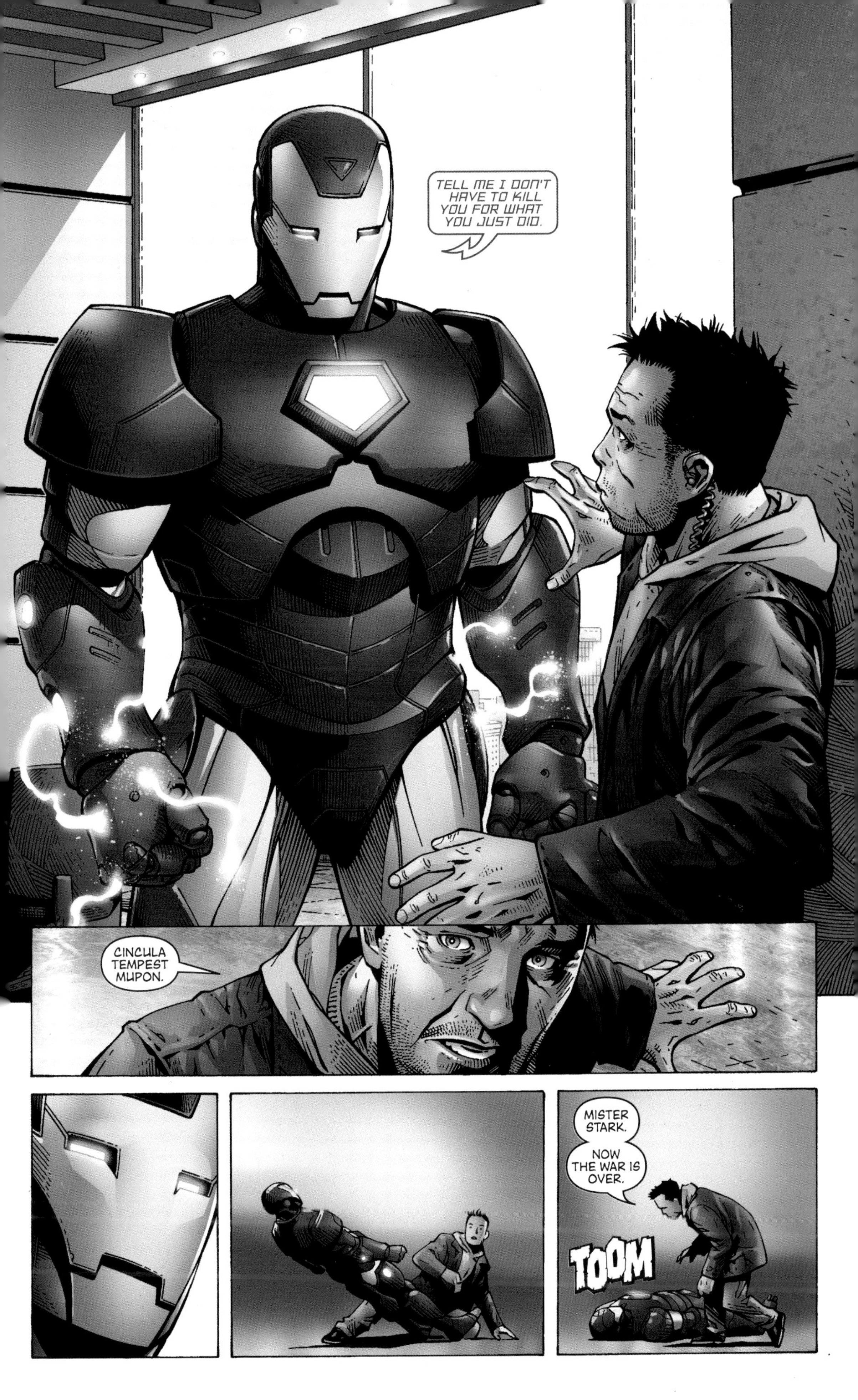
TELL ME I DON'T HAVE TO KILL YOU FOR WHAT YOU JUST DID.
CINCULA TEMPEST MUPON.
MISTER STARK.
NOW THE WAR IS OVER.
TOOM

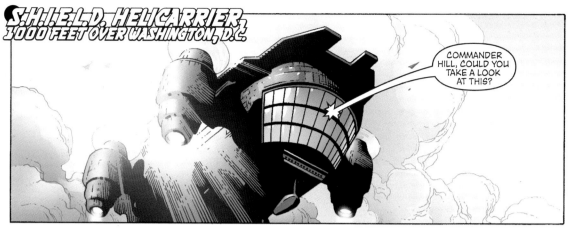

COMMANDER HILL, COULD YOU TAKE A LOOK AT THIS?

WHAT IS THAT?

WE INTERCEPTED A NEW YORK CITY POLICE SCANNER REPORT THAT SAID THE S.H.I.E.L.D. GUARD UNIT STATIONED OUTSIDE AVENGERS TOWER WAS DOWN.

DOWN?

BUT WE JUST CALLED IN AND THEY RESPONDED FINE.

AVENGERS TOWER GUARD, REPORT IN.

LET ME TALK TO THEM.

NOTHING TO REPORT. EVERYTHING IS FINE DOWN HERE.

THE POLICE SCANNER SAID YOU GUYS WERE DOWN.

NOTHING TO REPORT. EVERYTHING IS FINE DOWN HERE.

PULL UP A SATELLITE.

TIGHTER.

MUCH TIGHTER.

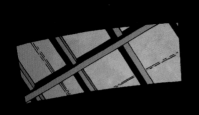
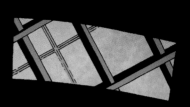

WHAT DID YOU *THINK* I WAS GOING TO DO, MR. STARK?

DID YOU THINK I WAS JUST GOING TO LET THIS GO ON?

THING IS--I BET YOU DIDN'T EVEN *CONSIDER* WHAT I WOULD THINK ABOUT THIS.

OR RHODES OR ANY OF US.

WE DEDICATED OUR *LIVES* TO YOU, MAN.

FOR YOU? NO.

FOR *IRON MAN.*

FOR THE *AVENGERS.*

FOR THE *IDEAL.* IT MEANT *EVERYTHING* TO ME. IT-IT--

AND YOU WENT-- AND-AND-AND-AND YOU JUST *COMPLETELY* TURNED AND DID AN ABOUT-FACE ON ME.

I WOULD *NEVER* HAVE AGREED TO USE MY DESIGNS TO ATTACK *CAPTAIN AMERICA.*

I WOULD *NEVER* HAVE SAID YES TO THIS.

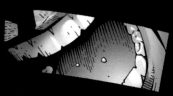

NEVER!

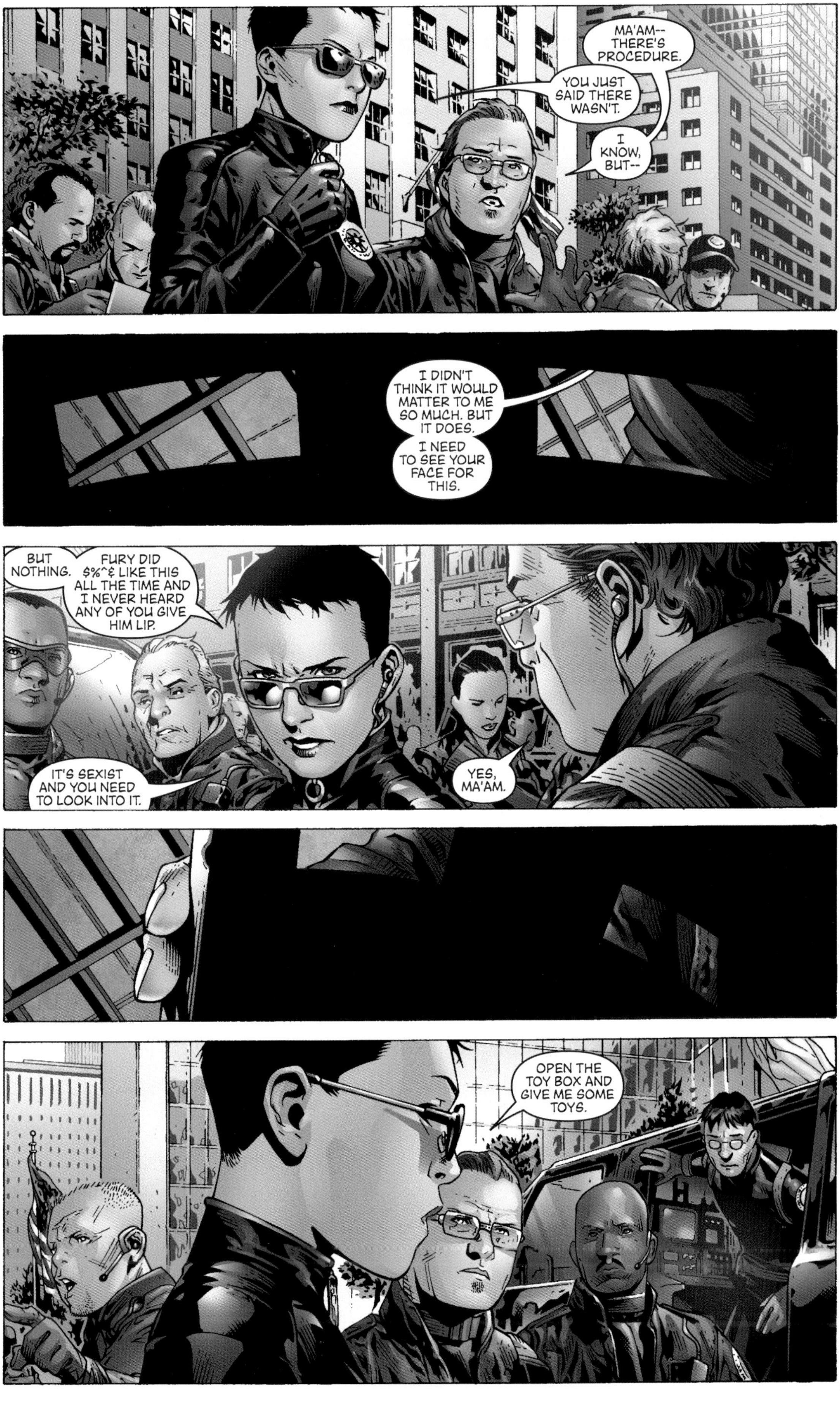
MA'AM-- THERE'S PROCEDURE.
YOU JUST SAID THERE WASN'T.
I KNOW, BUT--
I DIDN'T THINK IT WOULD MATTER TO ME SO MUCH. BUT IT DOES.
I NEED TO SEE YOUR FACE FOR THIS.
BUT NOTHING.
FURY DID $%^& LIKE THIS ALL THE TIME AND I NEVER HEARD ANY OF YOU GIVE HIM LIP.
IT'S SEXIST AND YOU NEED TO LOOK INTO IT.
YES, MA'AM.
OPEN THE TOY BOX AND GIVE ME SOME TOYS.

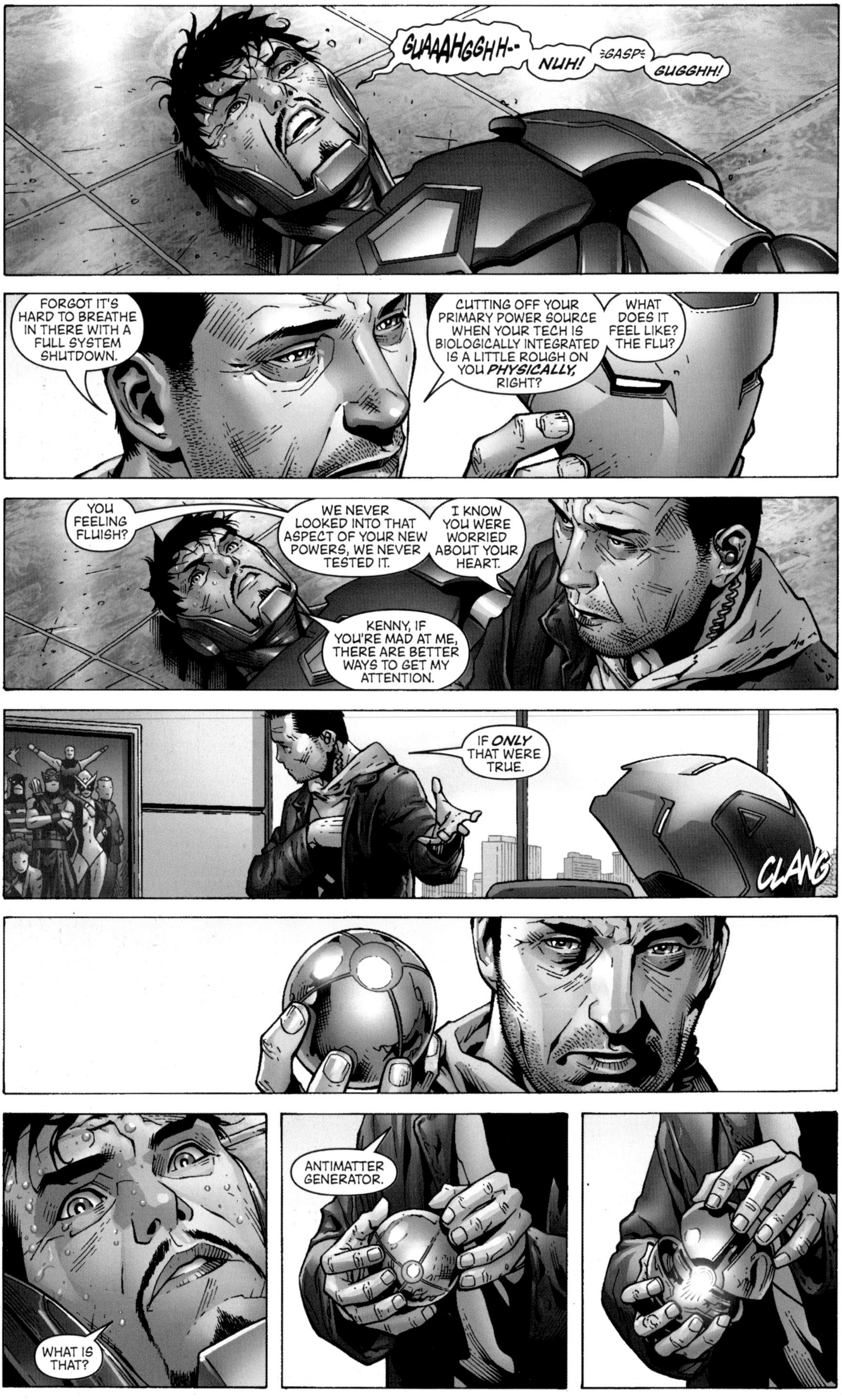

GUAAAHGGHH--
NUH!
GASP
GUGGHH!
FORGOT IT'S HARD TO BREATHE IN THERE WITH A FULL SYSTEM SHUTDOWN.
CUTTING OFF YOUR PRIMARY POWER SOURCE WHEN YOUR TECH IS BIOLOGICALLY INTEGRATED IS A LITTLE ROUGH ON YOU PHYSICALLY, RIGHT?
WHAT DOES IT FEEL LIKE? THE FLU?
YOU FEELING FLUISH?
WE NEVER LOOKED INTO THAT ASPECT OF YOUR NEW POWERS, WE NEVER TESTED IT.
I KNOW YOU WERE WORRIED ABOUT YOUR HEART.
KENNY, IF YOU'RE MAD AT ME, THERE ARE BETTER WAYS TO GET MY ATTENTION.
IF ONLY THAT WERE TRUE.
CLANG
WHAT IS THAT?
ANTIMATTER GENERATOR.

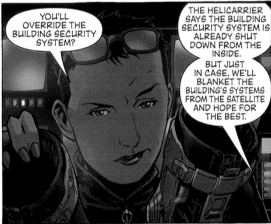

YOU REMEMBER THIS PIECE?

IT'S THE MATTER REVERSAL PROCESSOR THAT YOU WOULDN'T LET ME BUILD.

I BUILT IT ANYHOW, AND THIS BUILDING IS GOING TO DISAPPEAR.

FSSSS

THE PHYSICAL SPACE AND MATTER THAT MAKES UP THIS BUILDING IS GOING TO FOLD IN ON ITSELF UNTIL THERE'S NOTHING LEFT TO FOLD INTO.

AND THEN WHEN PEOPLE LOOK OUT THEIR WINDOWS AND SEE THE AVENGERS TOWER IS GONE FROM WHERE IT ONCE STOOD...

...MAYBE *THEN* THEY'LL STOP WITH THIS *"WHOSE SIDE ARE YOU ON?"* CRAP.

BECAUSE YOU'LL *HAVE* NO SIDES.

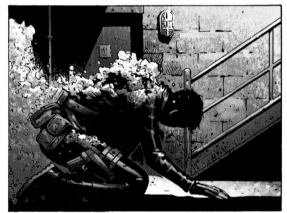

IT TAKES A MINUTE TO HEAT UP.

BUT IT WORKS.

I KNOW BECAUSE MY GARAGE IS NO LONGER WITH US.

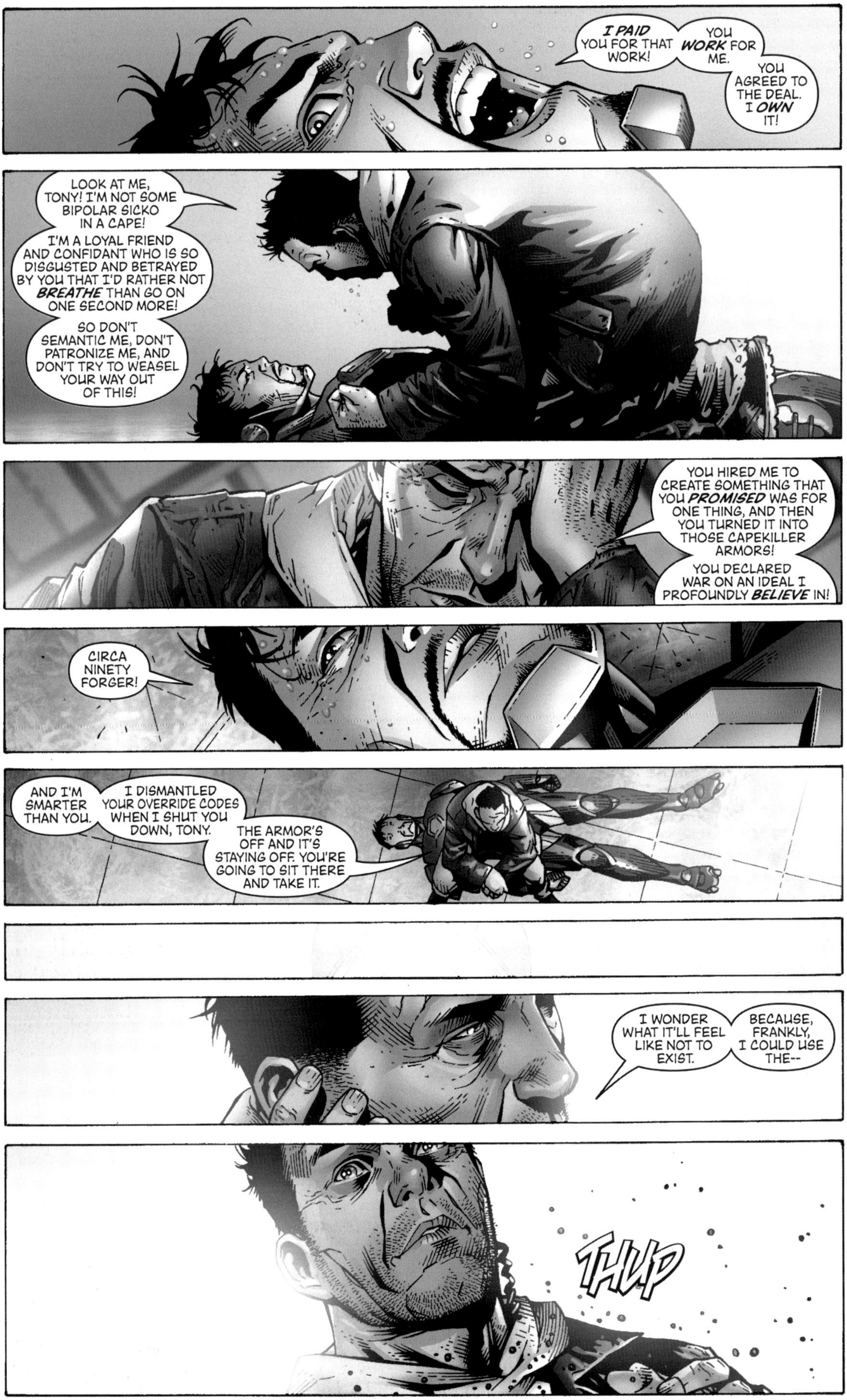
I PAID YOU FOR THAT WORK!
YOU WORK FOR ME.
YOU AGREED TO THE DEAL. I OWN IT!
LOOK AT ME, TONY! I'M NOT SOME BIPOLAR SICKO IN A CAPE!
I'M A LOYAL FRIEND AND CONFIDANT WHO IS SO DISGUSTED AND BETRAYED BY YOU THAT I'D RATHER NOT BREATHE THAN GO ON ONE SECOND MORE!
SO DON'T SEMANTIC ME, DON'T PATRONIZE ME, AND DON'T TRY TO WEASEL YOUR WAY OUT OF THIS!
YOU HIRED ME TO CREATE SOMETHING THAT YOU PROMISED WAS FOR ONE THING, AND THEN YOU TURNED IT INTO THOSE CAPEKILLER ARMORS!
YOU DECLARED WAR ON AN IDEAL I PROFOUNDLY BELIEVE IN!
CIRCA NINETY FORGER!
AND I'M SMARTER THAN YOU.
I DISMANTLED YOUR OVERRIDE CODES WHEN I SHUT YOU DOWN, TONY.
THE ARMOR'S OFF AND IT'S STAYING OFF. YOU'RE GOING TO SIT THERE AND TAKE IT.
I WONDER WHAT IT'LL FEEL LIKE NOT TO EXIST.
BECAUSE, FRANKLY, I COULD USE THE--
THUP

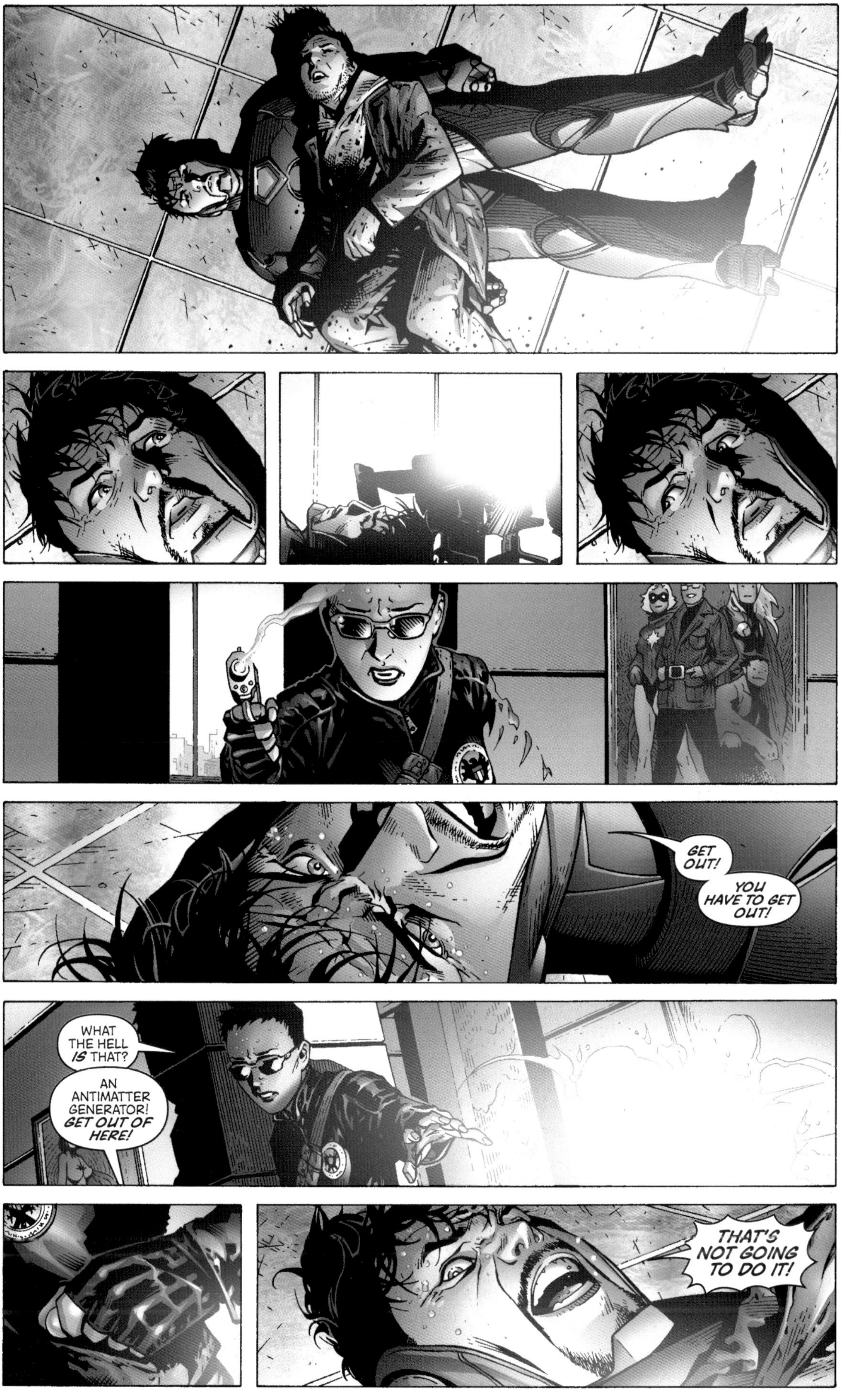
GET OUT!
YOU HAVE TO GET OUT!
WHAT THE HELL *IS* THAT?
AN ANTIMATTER GENERATOR! *GET OUT OF HERE!*
THAT'S NOT GOING TO DO IT!

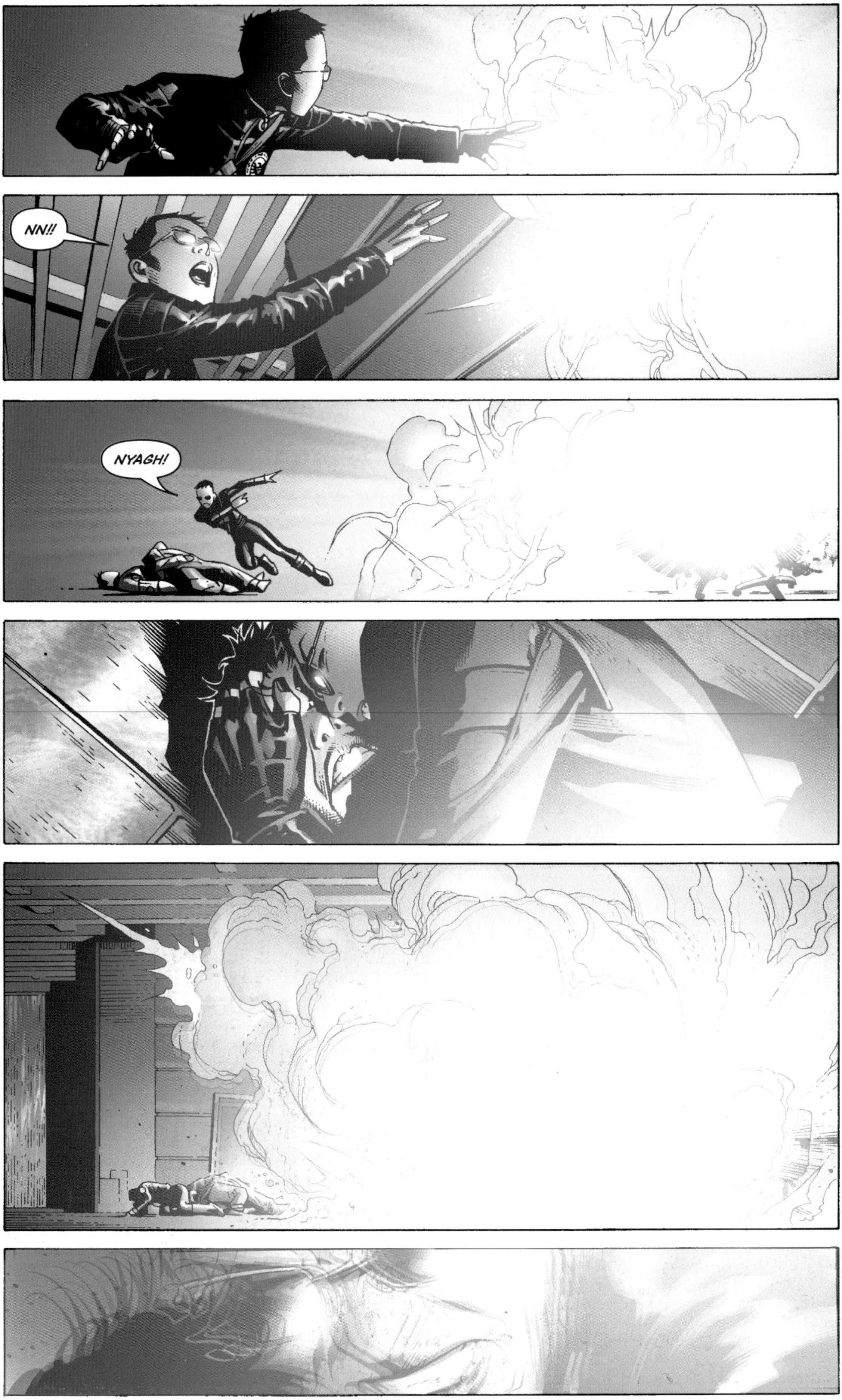
NN!!
NYAGH!

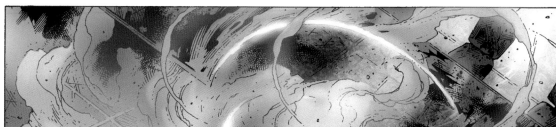

YOU OKAY?

NO.

OH MY GOD! TONY!

MED TEAM, WE NEED AN EVAC FOR JARVIS.

WHAT HAPPENED?

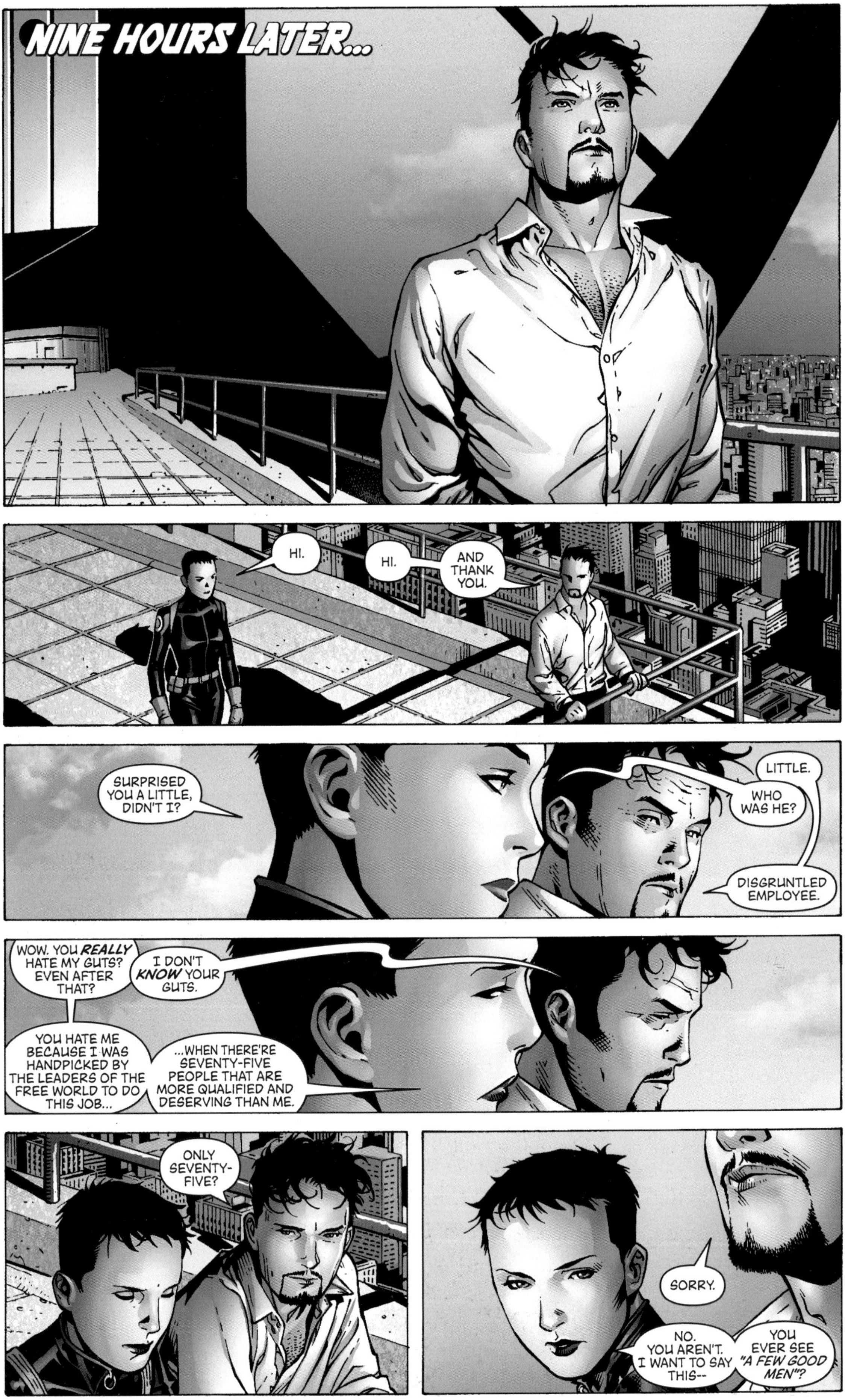
NINE HOURS LATER...
HI.
HI.
AND THANK YOU.
SURPRISED YOU A LITTLE, DIDN'T I?
LITTLE.
WHO WAS HE?
DISGRUNTLED EMPLOYEE.
WOW. YOU *REALLY* HATE MY GUTS? EVEN AFTER THAT?
I DON'T *KNOW* YOUR GUTS.
YOU HATE ME BECAUSE I WAS HANDPICKED BY THE LEADERS OF THE FREE WORLD TO DO THIS JOB...
...WHEN THERE'RE SEVENTY-FIVE PEOPLE THAT ARE MORE QUALIFIED AND DESERVING THAN ME.
ONLY SEVENTY-FIVE?
SORRY.
NO. YOU AREN'T. I WANT TO SAY THIS--
YOU EVER SEE *"A FEW GOOD MEN"*?

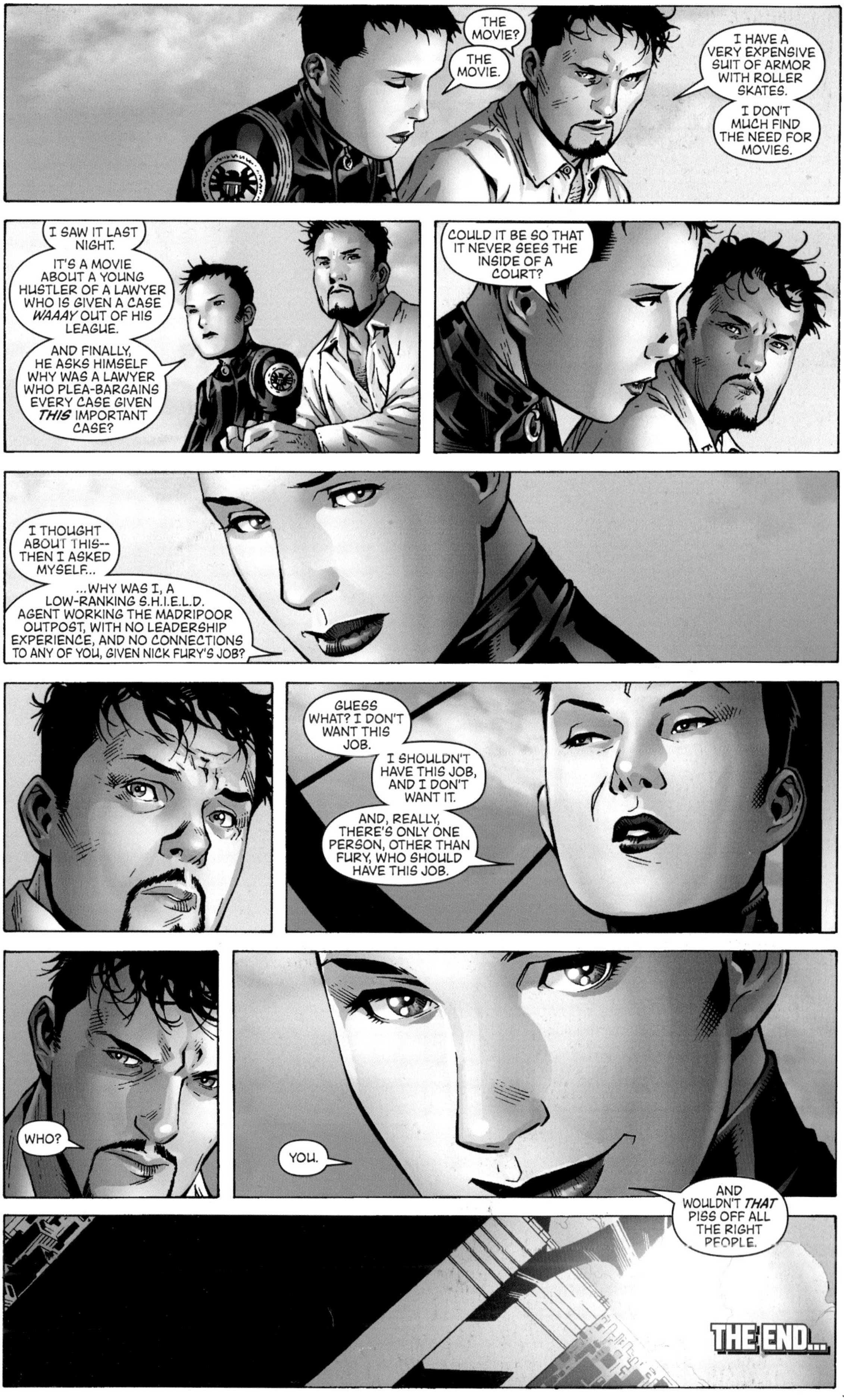
THE MOVIE?
THE MOVIE.
I HAVE A VERY EXPENSIVE SUIT OF ARMOR WITH ROLLER SKATES.
I DON'T MUCH FIND THE NEED FOR MOVIES.
I SAW IT LAST NIGHT.
IT'S A MOVIE ABOUT A YOUNG HUSTLER OF A LAWYER WHO IS GIVEN A CASE *WAAAY* OUT OF HIS LEAGUE.
AND FINALLY, HE ASKS HIMSELF WHY WAS A LAWYER WHO PLEA-BARGAINS EVERY CASE GIVEN *THIS* IMPORTANT CASE?
COULD IT BE SO THAT IT NEVER SEES THE INSIDE OF A COURT?
I THOUGHT ABOUT THIS-- THEN I ASKED MYSELF...
...WHY WAS I, A LOW-RANKING S.H.I.E.L.D. AGENT WORKING THE MADRIPOOR OUTPOST, WITH NO LEADERSHIP EXPERIENCE, AND NO CONNECTIONS TO ANY OF YOU, GIVEN NICK FURY'S JOB?
GUESS WHAT? I DON'T WANT THIS JOB.
I SHOULDN'T HAVE THIS JOB, AND I DON'T WANT IT.
AND, REALLY, THERE'S ONLY ONE PERSON, OTHER THAN FURY, WHO SHOULD HAVE THIS JOB.
WHO?
YOU.
AND WOULDN'T *THAT* PISS OFF ALL THE RIGHT PEOPLE.
THE END...

THE NEW AVENGERS®

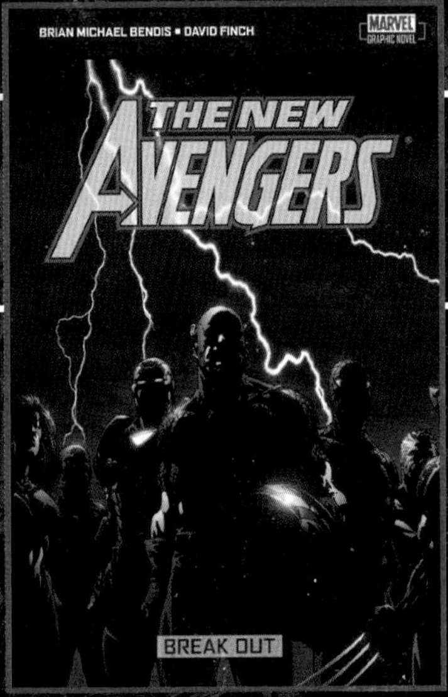
BRIAN MICHAEL BENDIS • DAVID FINCH
MARVEL GRAPHIC NOVEL
THE NEW AVENGERS
BREAK OUT

New Avengers Volume 1: Breakout
Collecting *New Avengers #1-6*
ISBN: 978-1-905239-14-6
£9.99

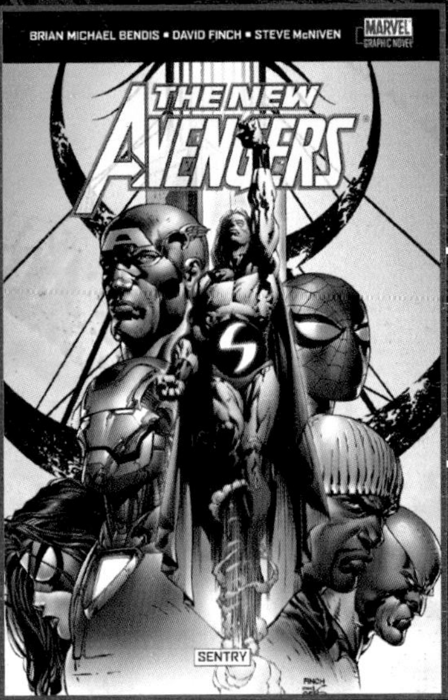
BRIAN MICHAEL BENDIS • DAVID FINCH • STEVE McNIVEN
MARVEL GRAPHIC NOVEL
THE NEW AVENGERS
SENTRY

New Avengers Volume 2: Sentry
Collecting *New Avengers #7-13*
ISBN: 978-1-905239-23-8
£11.99

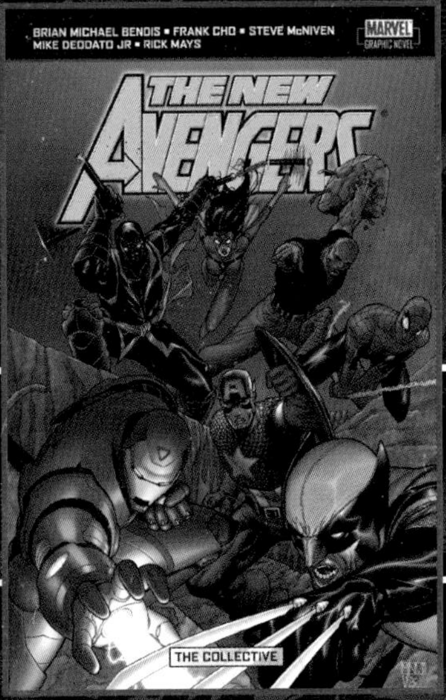
BRIAN MICHAEL BENDIS • FRANK CHO • STEVE McNIVEN
MIKE DEODATO JR • RICK MAYS
MARVEL GRAPHIC NOVEL
THE NEW AVENGERS
THE COLLECTIVE

New Avengers Volume 3: The Collective
Collecting *New Avengers #14-20* &
Giant Sized Spider-Woman #1
ISBN: 978-1-905239-68-9
£11.99

MARVEL® MAKE MINE MARVEL!